urban disciples

A Beginner's Guide to Serving God in the City

Jenell Williams Paris
Margot Owen Eyring

Judson Press
Valley Forge

Urban Disciples: A Beginner's Guide to Serving God in the City

© 2000 by Judson Press, Valley Forge, PA 19482–0851

Unless otherwise indicated, Bible quotations in this volume are from the New Revised Standard Version Bible, copyright © 1989, by the division of Christian Education of the National Council of the Churches of Christ in the United States of America.
Also quoted in this book is the Holy Bible, New International Version (NIV), copyright © 1973, 1978 by the International Bible Society, used by permission of Zondervan Bible Publishers.

Library of Congress Cataloging-in-Publication Data

Paris, Jenell Williams.
       Urban disciples : a beginner's guide to serving God in the city / Jenell Williams Paris and Margot Owen
Eyring.
                         p. cm.
       Includes bibliographical references
       ISBN 0–8170–1367–9 (pbk. : alk. paper)
       1. City churches. 2. City missions. I. Eyring, Margot Owen. II. Title.

BV637 .P37 2000
253'.091—dc21   00–037090

Printed in the U.S.A.

06 05 04 03 02 01 00

10 9 8 7 6 5 4 3 2 1

Contents

Foreword

BRINGING OUTSIDERS TO THE INNER CITY IS A COMPLICATED business, especially here in the United States. To cross cultures in this country is often to put oneself at risk spiritually and emotionally, if not always physically, and it is also to risk harming others out of misunderstanding and ignorance, if not always out of arrogance. Still, we do it all the time. There is something alluring about the American inner city—especially for evangelical Christians, something more than a simple desire to share the gospel—which draws us there again and again.

Whether that something is curiosity or guilt, missionary zeal or cultural imperialism, a promise of adventure or a quest for meaning, or some strange combination of them all, I do not know. I suspect it varies from person to person. Regardless, the simple fact is that nonurban evangelical Christians just keep coming to the inner city.

Mostly, they come on short-term missions trips, aiming to do a lot of good in a little time, the same way I came myself more than twenty years ago. That they mean well, just as I meant well, practically goes without saying. Unfortunately, when you come to the inner city, good intentions are not enough. You need to know what you are doing here.

Jenell Williams Paris and Margot Owen Eyring do not know what you are doing here (or there, as the case may be). What they do know is how to help you and your group figure that out for yourselves, by the grace of God. If you are looking for a book full of answers, then you will have to look elsewhere, but if you are looking for a book full of the right kinds of questions, here it is.

I wish I had asked these kinds of questions when I first came to the inner-city, but my nonurban Christian friends and I were too busy "saving" everybody to stop and think. Looking back now, I realize that we did a lot of damage along the way, harming the very people we had come to help. For one thing, we were convinced that we were God's gift to poor people, never once considering that they might be God's gift to us. We had no respect for our community. We had no sense of history. We figured that being better off was a sure sign that we were better, period.

As big as our egos were, our gospel was just that small. We aimed to save souls, not people. Blind to the poverty and injustice all around us, we offered folks simple solutions without even pausing to consider their very complicated problems. After all, the only Kingdom we were really interested in was heaven. To us, holistic ministry meant that you gave all four spiritual laws in each and every gospel presentation. And so we did.

Now I work with Mission Year, which is the antithesis of those early ministry experiences, and for which this workbook was first designed. Simply stated, Mission Year recruits Christian people eighteen to twenty-nine years of age from all over North America to join teams that live and work together in a poor urban neighborhood. As "members" of a strong local church, they reach out to their neighbors in a variety of practical ways. Besides church participation, these young people's weekly routine is devoted to community service (in public schools, hospitals, shelters, and other agencies) and neighborhood outreach, along with ongoing ministry training, team building, and daily personal devotions. There is no place for hit-and-run evangelism. This is informed, respectful, street-level stuff, with a real premium on understanding the city and learning how to build authentic relationships there, for the sake of the kingdom of God.

In many ways, Mission Year is our best answer so far to the questions that Jenell and Margot have posed so carefully in this book, questions that I believe every nonurban Christian should ask as he or she comes to the inner city. Your answers may be different, of course, and mine may change over time. As long as we ask them, however, we will know what we are doing in the inner city. We are learning to love God. We are learning to love one another. We are learning that nothing else really matters in the end.

I have learned much about these things from Jenell Williams Paris and Margot Owen Eyring, and so I am grateful to call them my friends. These are good women, who have done all kinds of good things in Jesus' name. This book is one more good thing, and I pray that it proves a blessing to you and your group. As Jenell and Margot know better than most, if you come right, the inner city is much more than worth the trip.

Bart Campolo
President, *Mission Year*

Preface

THIS WORKBOOK IS DESIGNED FOR URBAN MINISTRY TEAMS AND can be useful whether your group is planning, beginning, or in the midst of an urban ministry adventure. The exercises are adaptable for various kinds of groups, including church Bible study groups, college ministry groups, small groups, cell groups, urban plunge programs, short-term mission projects, urban ministry courses at seminaries and colleges, and people in the first years of long-term ministry.

This workbook was initially written as curriculum for Mission Year, a twelve-month urban Christian service program currently operating in Atlanta, Chicago, Philadelphia, and Oakland, California. We are thankful to Bart and Tony Campolo for their solicitation and support of our work. We revised the curriculum so that it can be adapted by many kinds of groups involved in various types of ministry projects.

I, Jenell Williams Paris, work as a professor of anthropology at Bethel College in St. Paul, Minnesota. I was raised in a suburb of Minneapolis, Minnesota, with little cross-cultural or urban experience. I spent the summers following my first and second years of college ministering to children and youth with KingdomWorks, an urban ministry organization that was then working in Philadelphia headed by Bart Campolo. I have invested in urban life as a neighbor, church member, and friend ever since those summers. My friendship with Bart Campolo has also continued since serving as a Kingdom-Works volunteer, a relationship that shaped my views on urban ministry and drew me into Mission Year as a curriculum developer.

I have lived in Minneapolis, St. Paul, Philadelphia, Washington, D.C., and Buffalo, New York, in both needy and privileged neighborhoods. My love for cities and my love of academics came together in graduate school as I studied cultural anthropology at American University, researching the inner-city neighborhood in Washington, D.C., where I lived for three and a half years. Currently, my husband and I live in north Minneapolis where I am active in my block club, neighborhood, and church.

I, Margot Owen Eyring, work as a member of the faculty team at the American Studies Program in Washington, D.C. Our vision is to connect biblical faith with public life and vocation. I searched for a part-time position so that I could also be available for involvement in my community and also have time for art and writing projects. For the past two and a half years, I have been the director of leadership and curriculum development with Building Bridges Youth Ministry. Other community work has included volunteering at a ministry for homeless men, working with a neighborhood collaborative, and serving as a deacon in my local church.

Moving almost twenty times and traveling to almost forty countries on five continents has well acquainted me with the processes of making transitions and of learning about new places. My approach to curriculum development and group learning tends to be holistic and often uses activities or approaches drawing from my cross-cultural experiences, catering insights, and artistic background, as well as my research about well-being and learning. My passion for helping people develop a more clear understanding of who they have been created to be and how God is calling them motivates me to invest in diverse settings with many unique people.

We, Jenell and Margot, lived together for over a year at Esther House, a Christian women's community house in Washington, D.C. We shared the house with four other women, working together to support one another's lives and the health of our neighborhood. The questions we raise about the city, spiritual formation, community, and transitions are ones we have lived and explored together. We wish the blessings of friendship to you and your community as you follow Christ together.

Introduction

GOD LOVES YOU. THAT MESSAGE IS TIMELESS AND UNIVERSAL AND is the heart of the gospel. In one sense, the Christian life is always the same: accepting God's love in our own lives and sharing God's love with others. Although its message remains constant, the gospel is alive. Depending on when, where, and to whom it is presented, will communicate different aspects of its truth to those who listen and indwell it. In the path of your discipleship, you may spend time in a city, a suburb, a corporation, a hospital, or hundreds of other places. As you learn about a new place—its ethos, its boundaries, its inhabitants, its dangers, and its blessings—you will develop better sensitivities to God's presence in your life and in that place. Likewise, your ministry to others will be more effective as you understand where they live and what matters most to them.

The lessons in this workbook are designed to guide your group through an urban adventure in a holistic, reflective, and respectful way. The activities are not for just "any city," or the idea of the city. Rather, they are about the city where God has brought you and your team. We borrow methods from cultural anthropology that help people be informed and strategic about learning a new place. Being intentional about learning shows respect for urban residents and leaders, and it also helps you be more relevant and collaborative in your outreach efforts. Lessons are not only about your city, however; they are also about you and your group. God wants you to care for others and to care for the city, but you are also responsible to be a steward of your own life. We use insights from many biblical traditions about spiritual formation to help you develop patterns of intentionality in your own spiritual journey. Since you are also functioning as a member of a team, we include lessons intended to nurture the important web of relationships in your group.

Participants in short-term mission efforts often say they received more than they gave, though their intent was to give and minister to others. Recipients of short-term mission efforts sometimes indicate they felt ignored or disrespected by overly confident missionaries who came with their own agendas and disrupted a community for a few days or weeks as they sought to help. These experiences are connected. A holistic approach to ministry can address the needs and concerns of both groups. Nurturing your own spiritual formation and the development of your group reminds you that even when you are helping others, you are also pursuing your own path of discipleship. This awareness should foster a healthy humility about what you have to offer others, and what you have to gain from them. Learning the city and partnering with God's people in the city prevents well-intentioned missionaries from being paternalistic or disrespectful. Those who are being served are more likely to feel empowered by this approach.

We believe learning should be fun, interactive, reflective, and inquisitive. Our workbook is based around important questions in five areas relevant to any urban ministry adventure: beginnings, learning and ministering in the city, growing in faith, building community together, and endings. Most of the questions could be answered by a six-year-old, a sixteen-year-old, or a sixty-year-old. We hope you engage the questions and continue to develop your answers throughout life. We do not want you to know just what we believe; rather, we want you to discover, shape, and confirm what you believe. Lessons are designed to empower and to equip you to live as a disciple of Christ in the world—specifically, in a city. Empowerment comes from experiencing and believing God's love for you and believing through faith that your existence and your actions matter to God. Equipping comes from developing the skills and disciplines of spirituality, anthropology, relationship-building, and ministry. These skills and disciplines can enable you to be more informed and reflective about how your personal and group decisions and actions contribute to the kingdom of God.

We hope this workbook creates a structure and a space for you to learn and that your learning comes alive as you draw on your personal experience and the expertise of those in your city. Feel free to adapt activities to your group's needs and work to make the questions and answers your own. We do not offer a single method, theology, or answer to the complex issues surrounding urban ministry. God is bigger than we are, so we don't presume to have the authoritative answers to complex questions. We do believe Jesus loves you and wants you to love God and others. This is one truth we hope you will come to believe and live even more deeply.

Using the Workbook

Lessons are designed to fit a multiple-week Bible study, a short-term mission project, a semester-long class, or a quarter-long Sunday school. Each lesson stands on its own, and lessons may be used in any order. However, your group, or group leader, should decide which lessons are most relevant for your group and arrange them accordingly.

If your group is planning or beginning an urban ministry adventure, we suggest you begin with lessons one through three. The lessons in the Beginnings unit raise foundational questions in three areas, including a process of learning more about the city, about your own spiritual formation, and about your group dynamics. In the midst of a project, groups or leaders may choose from lessons in Units 2, 3, and 4 (Learning and Ministering in the City,

Growing in Faith, and Building Community Together). Lessons are ordered in a logical progression, and we suggest that you begin by choosing lessons from the beginning of each unit, moving between units, to learn about the city, yourselves, and your team in a holistic way. The last unit, Endings, is designed to facilitate your transition from the project back to home.

Each lesson has four main parts: Starter, Study, Application, and Prayer, and includes a Digging Deeper section for further exploration. As you get started, these suggestions will help you monitor session times.

60-minute session	90-minute session
Starter: 10 min.	Starter: 15 min.
Study: 25 min.	Study: 30 min.
Application: 15 min.	Application: 30 min.
Prayer: 10 min.	Prayer: 15 min.

You may use Digging Deeper if you have extra time in a session or if you want to explore the topic more thoroughly. Digging Deeper activities may last from 10 to 30 minutes. As your group develops its own style of learning, you may want to adapt how you allocate the time to best fit the needs of your group.

Each group member should bring a Bible, this workbook, and a pen or pencil to each session. Scripture quotations are from the New Revised Standard Version, unless otherwise indicated. Resources in the Appendixes may be used throughout your learning adventure. Growth in personal and team spirituality can be supported with Appendixes A and F; learning about a new city or neighborhood can be guided with Appendixes B, C, D, and E; your transitions to and from your mission experience can be understood more fully using Appendix G.

Facilitating Meetings

We recommend that your group identify a person to facilitate meetings. The facilitator could be your team leader or another person who has group facilitation skills. Depending on the maturity of your group, it may be appropriate to rotate this leadership role. If possible, we suggest that the facilitator participate in lessons, as well as assume the responsibility of guiding the group through each meeting.

Hints for the Facilitator:

- Prepare! Read each lesson before your group meets. Determine which questions and activities are most appropriate for your group. Allocate time to each lesson section to fit your group's meeting time. Take note of any supplies that will be needed. For some sessions, a phone book or city map will be helpful.

- **Get things started.** Encourage group members to attend meetings on time. Think about a possible group ritual to begin the time together. For example, invite someone to read the lesson's Scripture as an opening prayer. Be sure to point everyone to the correct page in the workbook.
- **Guide the group along.** Keep an eye on the clock, but also be sensitive to how much time the group needs to complete an activity. You may need to modify the allotted times as you guide your group through each activity, or you might adjust the format or requirements for an activity. As a group, make sure to discuss your unique approach to time (e.g., time-oriented vs. event-oriented) and respect the time commitment made by your group, whether your session is 45 minutes, 60 minutes, or more. Make transitions between activities so the group finishes at your agreed upon time.
- **Participate.** Your role as a facilitator is to move the session along, not to have all the answers. If a difficult situation, a tough question, or disagreements arise, it is not your job to "fix" the situation or to correct others. Encourage the group to reach consensus and address issues as they arise. Participate with them in the process.
- **Share responsibilities.** Various team members can provide supplies (pens, Bibles, etc.), bring snacks, keep group records, remind people of meetings, arrange transportation, or prepare the room for each meeting. Sharing responsibilities helps each person have more stake in the group and keeps the facilitator from assuming too many duties. Deciding how to divide up the responsibilities of your group can be a helpful team building activity.
- **Discuss expectations.** During the first or second meeting, discuss the shared expectations for meetings. Are meetings confidential? Can friends or relatives come? What kinds of communication are valued? What is your orientation to time?

These lesson plans are designed to be user-friendly. Good facilitation is necessary, but not sufficient to help the group learn in the most effective way. Encourage each member to come prepared to commit to the group and participate in the process. We hope that each member of your team will engage with each other and with the issues raised in such a way that each member grows personally, that the team becomes a more complete part of the body of Christ, and God's kingdom becomes more evident.

More Resources
- John S. Hoffman and George Peck, eds. *The Laity in Ministry.* Valley Forge, Pa.: Judson Press, 1984.
- Nathan W. Turner. *Leading Small Groups: Basic Skills for Church and Community Organizations.* Valley Forge, Pa.: Judson Press, 1996.

unit one

Beginnings

6/25/02 Tuesday
Ian

Lesson 1
Why am I here?

Then Jesus said to the Jews who had believed in him,
"If you continue in my word, you are truly my disciples;
and you will know the truth, and the truth will make you free."
—John 8:31–32

➜ Starter

Think about why you embarked on this urban mission experience. Share with your group what brought you here. Take notes in the space below. Develop a list of group members' motivations. (You may want to revisit this list when you do your evaluation at the end of your urban experience.)

The children's ministry
Living life to the full
Intimacy w/ Christ.

📖 Study

You may enter into this urban ministry experience with any number of different attitudes. Our hope is that your heart is full of humility and grace as you work with other members on your team and with the people you have come to serve.

Acts 2:42–47 describes a group of joyful, generous believers who shared their lives and resources in ways such that both Christians and non-Christians had their needs met. The story of Ananias and Sapphira in Acts 5:1–11 presents us with an example of how inappropriate motives and actions can hinder the work of believers. Although Ananias and Sapphira were doing a good thing to share their resources with others, unfortunately their intentions were not pure and they conspired together to misrepresent their generosity. They lied about how much they were giving and were struck down dead.

Divide into two groups. Have each group review one of these stories. Identify guidelines and cautions to remember as you think about your service to God. When both groups are done, share insights with each other.

Reputation/recognition vs. Relationship w/Christ
— what is more valuable to us?

Total dependance on God.
— Christian socialism?
— security in Christ — giving and recieving
— Out of the overflow of Christ's love

Application

In groups of two, answer the following questions.

- Which people do you identify with more, those in Acts 2 who had everything in common or those in Acts 5 who pretended to share all they had?

It's definately easier for me to share all that I have w/ people that I like and love. And I definitely get caught up in pretending to share all that I have w/people I don't really care for. Then there are those who I don't even bother to pretend I've given my all. So, I guess I would be able to relate to both stories.

- In what areas of your life is it easy for you to share yourself generously with others? In what areas of your life is it difficult to share yourself with others?

It's easier for me to share when I'm intimate w/Christ. When He's a big presence in my life I'm drawn to be more generous. (After retreats, prayer times, etc) It's hard for me to be generous when I'm going through a spiritually dry time. I become petty and immature in my thought and action.

- Have you ever misrepresented yourself to others to put yourself in a better light? If so, how and why?

Definitely! To impress people. Trying to put the best foot forward. To manipulate situations. To control relationships and how they're progressing. But in the end I have to be a sinner saved by grace— nothing more or less.

✝ **Prayer**

Pray for your partner. If possible, share areas for prayer with the larger group.

🧠 Digging Deeper

Think about your vision for what you want to become through this experience. In your journal, identify one or two specific goals that will help you fulfill your vision. Keep your goals smart! SMART goals are Specific, Measurable, Actionable, Realistic, and Time-limited. Clear, intentional steps will help you move toward your vision. See Appendix A for journaling suggestions you can use throughout your experience to help you realize your goals.

	SMART goals	Not-so-SMART goals
Specific	Pray five minutes each day.	Pray more.
Measurable	Lose five pounds.	Lose weight.
Actionable	Give one compliment a day.	Be a better person.
Realistic	Write one letter a week.	Write to everyone weekly.
Time-limited	For the next three weeks.	For the rest of my life.

Say at least 1 encouraging thing to each teammate each day w/ sincerity and without obligation.

More Resources

- Tad Dunne. *Spiritual Mentoring: Guiding People through Spiritual Exercises to Life Decisions.* San Francisco: HarperSanFrancisco, 1991.
- Gordon MacDonald. *Ordering Your Private World.* Nashville: Thomas Nelson, 1984.

Lesson 2
Why be in community?

Handwritten notes in top right margin:
Wednesday 6/26/02
Rachel.
- friend Josh in India
- desire to be like Christ not to be distracted by heat/tiredness

Two are better than one,
because they have a good reward for their toil.
For if they fall, one will lift up the other;
but woe to one who is alone and falls
and does not have another to help.
—Ecclesiastes 4:9–10

➡ Starter

This starter activity is a race. Divide up into teams of three or four people. Identify a "race course" between two chairs. Place a shirt or jacket beside one chair. The goal is for each team to start at the first chair and race to the second chair. Sit in the second chair, put on the shirt, and then race back to the first chair and sit on it. There is a catch. The team must function as one body. There must be only one pair of eyes (the other three people must be blindfolded), one mouth (the other mouths must be quiet), and two usable arms (not owned by the same person). The other arms cannot be used except to carry the members of the group who cannot walk. If there are four people in the group, then only five feet can touch the ground. This means one person must be carried! If there are three people in a group, only three feet can touch the ground. After the race, give the winning group a prize and talk about the experience.

- What did the groups do to be successful?

- What made the task difficult?

- What lessons about team work did you learn from this experience?

Lesson 2: Why be in community?

 **Study**

Read 1 Corinthians 12:1–31 out loud.

- What is the purpose of the different gifts?

  To function as a greater whole. No one has all the gifts. To be one body. To diversify the potential blessings. Life is good when things are different.

- What is the purpose of one body having many different parts?

  To be an encouragement to one another. To keep one another accountable. So we can do more things. We are all gifted/talented in different ways.

- What lessons do we learn in this passage about the relationships between the parts and the body? Were any of these truths experienced in "the race"?

  They have to function together in their differences not in their commonality. Giving/recieving to work toward the same goal.

- What implications do those lessons have for your team as you minister in this urban setting?

  Letting other people be strong/gifted is our backing/weakness. Mutual submission for the greater good. To encourage one another in having their strengths.

Application

Discuss the following questions together.

- Think about the metaphor of a body and how individual Christians are like body parts. What part of the body do you most identify with? Why?

  The eyes. — to observe and see tools at work and the need out there. To process what is seen.

- Think about your team and the "body parts" represented by group members. Are there any missing parts? What implications might this lack have on the group? What strengths does your particular team have? What benefits might your group receive from these particular strengths?

  The grunt worker. It requires the rest of us to pick up the slack. The strength is our commitment to the greater goal. Helps keep perspective and give grace when mistakes are made.

6

- Considering the uniqueness of your team, why might God have brought this particular group together?

To teach me what it means to love and to shepherd a group of people. To teach my heart to be more sensitive. To stretch me and make me more dependent on Christ. I need His strength, wisdom, and love to do what is laid out before me. He's been faithful in the past.

✚ **Prayer**

Many times, prayers focus only on what we have to say to God. But, in any relational communication, both parties should listen and speak. We are going to try to listen to God during this time of prayer. Being silent helps us to focus on God and what the Spirit might be saying to us.

Identify a leader who will be in charge of the time. Spend six minutes in silence together in God's presence. Allow the Lord to speak to your hearts. After the time of silence is over, share any insights that God gave you.

follow me. My yoke is easy and light. Cast all your cares upon me. My grace is sufficient for you. I will provide you w/ all you need. Be blessed, my child.

Digging Deeper

Brainstorm a list of blessings that may come from working and being together. Think of blessings that you probably would not experience if you were alone.

- *Not seeing one another grow.* — *encouragement*
- *>> Spirit will be upon us.* — *beauty in diversity*
- *Having different perspectives / schools of thought.* — *sharing life.*

More Resources

- Juan Carlos Ortiz. *Disciple.* Carol Steam, Ill.: Creation House, 1975.
- Paul D. Stanley and J. Robert Clinton. *Connecting: The Mentoring Relationships You Need to Succeed in Life.* Colorado Springs: Navpress, 1992.
- Lucibel Van Atta. *Women Encouraging Women.* Portland: Multnomah Press, 1987.

Lesson 3
Where are we in this city?

The LORD watches over all who love him,
but all the wicked he will destroy.
My mouth will speak the praise of the LORD,
and all flesh will bless his holy name forever and ever.
— Psalm 145:20,21

➜ Starter

Recognizing the ideas and perceptions that you bring with you to your ministry location can help you to be more sensitive to the new ideas and places you will encounter. Begin by talking with a partner about your own home and neighborhood. These places are important to keep in mind as you begin to experience and describe your "new city."

- Describe the house (or houses) where you grew up. What color was your house? Was there a grass lawn? A cement lawn? What was your bedroom like? What was your favorite thing about your house?

  Grew up in basically two houses. At first, various apartments. A lot of neighborhood kids. in a working class background. Then moved in 7th grade to a white collar neighborhood. With no street lights, 2 acre plots, no sidewalks, and little man-made ponds and lakes. My bedroom is great. (X) bed, TV, computer

- What was your neighborhood like? What was your favorite thing about living in your town, city, or suburb? Based on your first impressions, is this new city similar or different from where you grew up?

  This is way, way, way different than Barrington. There's so much observable pain and ugliness here. The brokenness is so apparent and in your face.

📖 Study

It is difficult to find your way in a city when you are unfamiliar with roads, neighborhoods, and landmarks. Even when geography is familiar, it is still a challenge to really see

8

and understand the area where you are doing ministry. This exercise is designed to help you learn more about the place where God has called you. You will draw maps and charts that will help you minister by increasing your knowledge of places, people, and resources.

- **Exploring.** (Optional) To begin, you may need to spend 30 minutes exploring the neighborhood by foot or by car. Divide into small teams of two or three. Observe as much as you can. Take notes about what stands out to you.

- **Mapping.** Post a piece of newsprint on the wall and begin to map your neighborhood or ministry target area. Begin with your church, ministry center, or a significant central landmark. Draw and label the streets surrounding it. Map neighborhood boundaries if you know them. Next, map major land divisions—rivers, railroads, subways, etc. Next, identify how land is used—residence, retail/commercial, churches, schools, banks, government buildings, shelters, restaurants. Go into as much detail as time and your memory allows.

- **Networking.** Begin a list of important contacts to accompany your map. What telephone numbers will you need as you minister? Think about adding local churches, police, emergency numbers, neighbors, and referral numbers (e.g., for shelters, churches, food banks, hospitals). Don't forget the numbers of the people on your team! Appendix B contains a form for important contacts. Photocopy this page and post it near a telephone if appropriate.

✎ Application

Walk around several blocks in the city together, in groups of four people or less. Pray silently as you go. Ask the Holy Spirit to provide opportunities to meet people and for insights about what may be happening spiritually in the area. When you return, update your map and discuss what you learned.

- What did you most notice on your walk?

- How is this neighborhood like, and how is it unlike the area where you grew up?

- What concerns you about the area? What encourages you?

- What is God already doing here?

✝ Prayer

Use your map as a reference to guide your prayer. Pray with your eyes open. Start praying for things in the center of the map and move out to the edges. Note any important concerns for continued prayer during your time in the city.

 Digging Deeper

Brainstorm a list of places to visit in the city. Think of places such as museums, government buildings, art galleries, universities, and notable restaurants or cafes. Make a specific plan with other group members to begin visiting some of these places. Appendix C is a "Learning Adventures" form that will help you organize and share your team's learning.

More Resources

- Ulf Hannerz. *Exploring the City: Inquiries Toward an Urban Anthropology.* New York: Columbia University Press, 1980.
- Robert Lupton. *Return Flight: Community Development Through Reneighboring Our Cities.* Atlanta: FCS Urban Ministries, 1993.
- John Perkins. *Beyond Charity: The Call to Christian Community Development.* Grand Rapids, Mich.: Baker Book House, 1993.

unit two

Learning and Ministering in the City

Lesson 4
How do we begin learning about this city?

Give instruction to the wise, and they will become wiser still;
teach the righteous and they will gain in learning.
—Proverbs 9:9

➜ Starter

Imagine a city expert is at your meeting. This person knows everything about this city's economy, history, people, neighborhoods . . . everything! What do you want to know? Develop three questions for this expert. Share your questions with each other. Keep these questions in mind as you develop your learning plan.

1. What is keeping this area from economic growth?

2. What were the causes of the deterioration of this neighborhood?

3. How can we, as individuals, make a lasting impact on this neighborhood.

 Study

In this study time, your group will develop a plan for learning about your city. Begin by brainstorming places and people to visit. Identify the questions you could pursue at each place. On the chart below, write down all suggestions without evaluating them. Later, you can pick and choose the options that best suit your group. After developing your list, compare it with the list in Appendix D, adding useful resources to your list.

Person or Place	Key Questions
local city representative	What are some changes that we are trying to implement.
local elementary school/ principal.	What area do the kids need the most help?
local high school principal	Where are the youth going? who are they growing up to be?
Average Neighbor	What is needed in this neighborhood? How can we serve your family?
Average youth	What do you want changed in your life and this neighborhood.

Application

Review the list that you brainstormed. Draw a star by the people and places that seem most important and most feasible for your group to visit. Volunteer as individuals, pairs, or small groups to explore one of the identified people or places. Appendix C includes a format for taking notes on these visits. As a group, set a meeting time when you will debrief your experiences and tell the others what you have learned. Consider developing a record-keeping system (e.g., collecting notes, newspapers, articles, other documents) in order to organize and remember the information you want to share with the group.

 Prayer

Beginning to learn about new areas and new people can be both exciting and intimidating or scary. It can be hard to know how to begin a conversation with people you don't know, or it can be hard to be open with strangers about how much you don't know. Spend two minutes in silence. Think about your current knowledge of the city and what you would like to learn. How do you feel—challenged? confident? excited? afraid? nervous? disinterested? engaged? After a period of silence, speak to God about learning in this city. Ask God for help and confidence as you and your group take steps in learning about your new context. Ask one person to close the prayer time by reading this unit's opening Scripture, Proverbs 9:9, as a reminder that knowledge and wisdom come with learning.

Digging Deeper

Use a phone book to expand your options of places to visit and people to call. Generate a list of addresses and phone numbers that group members can use to meet new people and places. The government pages are often helpful for finding city offices. (Try looking under Mayor's Office, Chamber of Commerce, Office of Planning, Office of Tourism, Parks, Recreation, Libraries, etc.) The yellow pages can point you to restaurants, shops, and religious institutions in the area. You may network with your contacts in the community for ideas.

More Resources

- J. Daniel Hess. *The Whole World Guide to Culture Learning.* Yarmouth, Maine: Intercultural Press, 1994.
- James C. Perkins; Jean Alicia Elster, ed. *Building Up Zion's Walls: Ministry for Empowering the African American Family.* Valley Forge, Pa.: Judson Press, 1999.
- Harold J. Recinos. *Hear the Cry! An Urban Pastor Challenges the Church.* Louisville, Ky.: Westminster/John Knox Press, 1989.

Lesson 5
Does God love this city?

God is in the midst of the city;
it shall not be moved;
God will help it when the morning dawns.
—Psalm 46:5

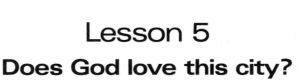 **Starter**

Work as a group and brainstorm a list of words that you associate with the words "city" and "country." Take notes in the chart below. Discuss together what you heard.

City	Country

- What do you notice about each list?

- What might your lists suggest about your group's preconceptions about urban and rural life?

Study and Application

This learning exercise focuses on prayer as an action step in ministry. Praying for yourself, your team, and specific people and places in your city are essential parts of ministry. Prayer is doing ministry, not just preparing for ministry. First, study a "big picture" view of what the Bible says about cities. For each Scripture, answer the questions on the chart. Then think carefully about what Scripture reveals about God's perspective on *this* city.

	Study What does this passage tell us about God's perspective on justice and the city?	**Application** Insights about God's perspective on *our* group in *this* city?
Isaiah 64:10–12		
Psalm 82:1–8		
Isaiah 61:1–4		
Habakkuk 2:6–14	God will destroy anything that's been gain unjustly. His glory will prevail	We must be upright in our endeavors.
Revelation 22:1–5	There will no longer be a curse.	The hope that fuels us

16

✝ Prayer

Pray a "popcorn" prayer. Encourage every team member to "pop up" and speak brief sentence or word prayers. Pray using the insights you gained from exploring God's perspective on the city. Pray using the information you have already learned about this new city. For example, pray by name for this city, its leaders, its neighborhoods, its streets, its churches, and other aspects of the city you are learning to care about. If you don't know specifics yet, use a phone book and call out names of businesses, churches, and streets. Pray for yourselves to have God's perspective on this city.

🗣 Digging Deeper

Brainstorm ways to share God's love for the city with others. Think about your family, your church, your local Christian radio or TV stations, or Christian magazines that you read. How can you influence people to love the city as God does?

More Resources

- John E. Kyle, ed. *Urban Mission: God's Concern for the City.* Downers Grove, Ill.: InterVarsity Press, 1988.
- Robert Lupton. *Theirs Is the Kingdom: Celebrating the Gospel in Urban America.* San Francisco: Harper & Row, 1989.
- Harold J. Recinos. *Jesus Weeps: Global Encounters on our Doorstep.* Nashville: Abingdon Press, 1992.
- Randy White. *Journey to the Center of the City.* Downers Grove, Ill.: InterVarsity Press, 1997.

Lesson 6
What is God's vision for this city?

Pray for the peace of Jerusalem:
"May they prosper who love you.
Peace be within your walls,
and security within your towers."
For the sake of my relatives and friends
I will say, "Peace be within you."
For the sake of the house of the LORD our God,
I will seek your good.
—Psalm 122:6–9

➜ Starter

Think about the most beautiful image you have of a city. Your image can be one you've actually seen, or something you have imagined. Share your ideas with your group.

📖 Study

Jerusalem is the most important city in the Bible. God ordained Jerusalem as the capital of David's kingdom. It was fortified by Solomon and later was captured and pillaged by several kings. The Israelites worked to rebuild and restore Jerusalem. Jesus first preached the gospel in Jerusalem and was crucified there. The Pentecostal revival happened in Jerusalem. The Bible's final prophecies use Jerusalem as a metaphor for the future coming of God's kingdom. This study guides you through the Old and New Testaments, looking at several biblical themes related to Jerusalem. You may work through all the passages together, or work in smaller groups and later share your answers.

Lesson 6: What is God's vision for this city?

- How do the biblical writers describe God's love for Jerusalem?

  Psalm 122

  Isaiah 62:1–7,12

- Sometimes destructive forces worked against the city, and the people and leaders of the city sinned against each other. What does the Bible say about sin in Jerusalem?

  Psalm 55:9–11

  Isaiah 40:1–2

  Jeremiah 5:1–6

- Jerusalem was an important city in Jesus' life. He traveled there as a child and he worshiped at the temple there during his life. He was arrested just east of the city, put on trial in Jerusalem, and was crucified just west of the city. What do the following Scriptures say about Jesus' view of Jerusalem?

Matthew 16:21

Luke 19:28–44

Luke 24:45–49

- The book of Revelation refers to the "New Jerusalem," a heavenly city coming down to earth. Revelation uses Jerusalem as a metaphor for the future coming of God's kingdom in its fullness. How does the author of Revelation describe God's coming kingdom? Why do you think he uses Jerusalem as an image for the end times?

Revelation 21:1–4

Revelation 21:9–14

 **Application**

Think about the city where you are serving. Discuss together the following questions in light of what you learned about Jerusalem.

- What does God's care for Jerusalem show about God's love for this city?

- Look back at your notes about sin in Jerusalem. Do you see similar sins in this city today? What are similarities or differences that you note?

- Think about the images of the New Jerusalem in the book of Revelation. What might God's kingdom look like in this city?

- What might be God's vision for this city?

✛ Prayer

Spend time in meditative prayer as you listen to one person read Psalm 122. It is a psalm of love for the city. The psalmist prays for the peace of the city and looks ahead to God's redemption. Try to empathize with the emotions and passion of the psalmist.

🗣 Digging Deeper

Work together to memorize Psalm 122. Carrying this psalm in your heart may help you remember God's love and hope for the city as you experience similar emotions.

More Resources

- Cain Hope Felder and Tony Campolo. *Lift Every Voice: The Bible in an Age of Diversity.* Valley Forge, Pa.: Judson Press, nd. Videocassette.
- Ray Bakke. *A Theology as Big as the City.* Downers Grove, Ill.: InterVarsity Press, 1997.
- John M. Perkins, ed. *Restoring At-Risk Communities.* Grand Rapids, Mich.: Baker Book House, 1995.

Lesson 7
What's right in this city?

*Thus says the LORD of hosts: Old men and old women shall
again sit in the streets of Jerusalem, each with staff in hand
because of their great age. And the streets of the city shall be full
of boys and girls playing in its streets.*
—*Zechariah 8:4–5*

 Starter

Often when nonurban Christians enter a city, the first things they see are poverty, graffiti, and homeless people. They think of ministry in terms of problems: How can we address poverty? How can we clean up this neighborhood? How can we help the homeless?

Even though there are problems to solve, we need to begin by seeing strengths in the city. God created the city and its residents. God has been alive and active in the city long before your group even thought about developing an urban ministry. If your group focuses on problems and sees your resources as providing the solutions, urban residents and leaders are likely to see you as arrogant and paternalistic. If you see God and God's people in the city, you can partner with them and build on existing strengths as you work to solve problems. If you build partnerships and alliances in the city first and then offer your resources, your efforts are more likely to be accepted as a positive contribution of collaboration.

Take a ten-minute walk around the area where you are ministering. If you are doing this lesson in an area different from your ministry area, that's fine. The goal is to focus on learning to see assets. Walk around the area. Look for things that are healthy—people, stores, schools, agencies, landscaping, parks, etc. As you are walking, talk about what's working. When you return, write some notes in the space below to remind you about what you saw.

 **Study**

Read John 4:1–42 using three readers for the three "parts": a narrator, Jesus, and the woman at the well. After reading the passage, divide into groups of two or three and discuss the following questions:

- What barriers did Jesus face in this story?

- How did he move beyond those barriers to connect with the woman?

- What were the implications of his actions for all those involved?

- What barriers do we face as we seek to meet the needs of those in this city? How can we move beyond these barriers?

- What principles can we glean from this story?

Share your answers with the larger group.

 Application

Develop the chart on pages 26–27 and use it to discuss your ministry area or the city you are targeting. Rely on your notes and be as specific as you can in answering the following questions:

- What's working? Which people, agencies, places, or policies are making positive contributions in this area?

- What's not working? Which people, places, buildings, behaviors, policies, or other issues are problems in the area?

- How can we be part of the solution? How can we connect with healthy people and institutions to make a positive difference?

 **Prayer**

Read Colossians 1:15–17 out loud. Ask God to help you see God's divine creative work in the city. Pray that your group will learn to see the city as God sees it, with strengths as well as weaknesses.

 **Digging Deeper**

Using the chart on pages 26–27, reflect on your upbringing. What made your neighborhood work well? Think about government, schools, churches, hospitals, and your family and neighbors. How might your personal expeiences help or hinder you in this city?

More Resources

- Karen Jones Bernstine, ed. *Church and Family Together: A Congregational Manual for Black Family Ministry.* Valley Forge, Pa.: Judson Press, 1996.
- Curtiss Paul DeYoung. *Reconciliation: Our Greatest Challenge—Our Only Hope.* Valley Forge, Pa.: Judson Press, 1997.
- Jonathan Kozol. *Amazing Grace: The Lives of Children and the Conscience of a Nation.* New York: Crown Publishers, Inc., 1995.
- Wallace Charles Smith. *The Church in the Life of the Black Family.* Valley Forge, Pa.: Judson Press, 1985.

Lesson 7: What's right in this city?

Study	What's working?	What's not working?
Churches		
Families		
Schools		
Hospitals and healthcare		
Government		
Arts and culture		
Sports and recreation		
Businesses		
Other		

Lesson 7: What's right in this city?

How can we be part of the solution?	How can your background help or hinder?

Lesson 8

Where is hope for the city?

Blessed be the God and Father of our Lord Jesus Christ!
By his great mercy he has given us a new birth into a living
hope through the resurrection of Jesus Christ from the dead,
and into an inheritance that is imperishable,
undefiled, and unfading, kept in heaven for you,
who are being protected by the power of God
through faith for a salvation
ready to be revealed in the last time.
—1 Peter 1:3–5

➡ Starter

Where have you seen hopelessness in this city? Where have you seen signs of hope? Make a brief list.

Hope	Hopelessness

Which list was easier for you to make? Share your answer and your list with your team.

 **Study**

Have at least two different people read Ephesians 1 out loud from different translations of the Bible. Take notes on what Paul says about hope. Work in pairs on the following questions.

- What is the "hope to which [God] has called you" (Ephesians 1:17–19)?

- What does Paul say about Jesus in this chapter?

- What hope does faith in Christ offer?

Look back at your notes about Ephesians 1. What else did you learn? Discuss insights with your entire team.

Application

Imagine a friend or family member wrote to you and asked, "I admire you for what you're trying to do in your urban outreach, but to be honest, I don't see the point. It's hopeless! There's trash everywhere, poverty, drugs, and crime. Where do you find hope?"

Spend at least ten minutes writing a response. Then, with a partner or group of three, read your letters out loud and discuss them.

Dear _____ ,

 ## Prayer

Read Ephesians 1:17–19 out loud. Meditate on God's promise of hope for those who believe in Jesus. Ask the Holy Spirit to reveal more of God's hope to you, your group, and to the city.

Digging Deeper

Think about your urban outreach or your plans for urban outreach. Think about your personal strengths and weaknesses in doing ministry. How might your experiences in the city deepen your hope? How might they challenge your hope? Discuss these questions with a partner or with the group.

More Resources

- Robert D. Carle and Louis A. DeCaro Jr., eds. *Signs of Hope in the City: Ministries of Community Renewal.* Valley Forge, Pa.: Judson Press, 1997.
- Harvie Conn. *Planting and Growing Urban Churches: From Dream to Reality.* Grand Rapids, Mich.: Baker Book House, 1997.
- Howard Thurman. *Jesus and the Disinherited.* New York: Abingdon/Cokesbury, 1949.

Lesson 9
Where is justice in the city?

He has told you, O mortal, what is good;
and what does the LORD require of you but to do justice,
and to love kindness, and to walk humbly with your God?
—Micah 6:8

Starter

Think of a person whom you consider to be just. What makes that person just? Share your answers with the group.

Study

Divide into three groups. Each group will work on one question. Take notes on each Scripture, and then develop an answer based on insights from all of the passages. Discuss your answers with the entire group.

- What is justice?

  Leviticus 19:15

  Deuteronomy 10:17–19

Isaiah 42:1–7

Romans 13:3–4

• Why is justice important to God?

Deuteronomy 32:4

Psalm 9:7–12

Isaiah 30:18

• What did Jesus say about justice? (In the original language, "righteousness" and "justice" are similar words).

Matthew 6:33

Luke 4:18–19

Luke 7:21–23

Application

In light of your previous insights about justice, discuss the following questions together. As you formulate answers, be specific about applying justice to your group, this city, and your ministry here.

- What does it mean to do justice?

- How is doing justice related to sharing the gospel? How are they different? How are they the same?

- What are some of the people or situations in this city that are just? How might your group partner with them to encourage their efforts?

- What are some of the main injustices you see in this city? How might your ministry address some of them?

 **Prayer**

Write one or two sentences using the word "justice." Read your sentences out loud as a prayer. Ask the Holy Spirit to make you more just people, and to help you make the world a more just place.

 Digging Deeper

Read Amos 5 out loud. Using the following chart, take notes on what Amos says about poverty, wealth, and justice. Discuss what you heard. What was Amos saying to the people of his time? What do his words mean for us today?

Poverty	Wealth	Justice

More Resources

- Curtiss Paul DeYoung. *Coming Together: The Bible's Message in an Age of Diversity.* Valley Forge, Pa.: Judson Press, 1995.
- David Ng, ed. *People on the Way: Asian North Americans Discovering Christ, Culture, and Community.* Valley Forge, Pa.: Judson Press. 1996.

unit three

Growing in Faith

Lesson 10
Who is Jesus?

In the beginning was the Word,
and the Word was with God,
and the Word was God.
He was in the beginning with God.
All things came into being through him,
and without him not one thing came into being.
What has come into being in him was life,
and the life was the light of all people.
The light shines in the darkness,
and the darkness did not overcome it.
—John 1:1–5

 **Starter**

Think about the most meaningful image of Jesus you have seen. It could be an artistic image, a person who images Jesus, a story, or any other image that is meaningful to you. Describe the image to your team and tell why it is powerful for you.

 **Study**

In the first century, people did not learn in classrooms with chairs in rows, with the students sitting and the teacher standing. In Jesus' time, when a teacher sat down, it was a sign that the teacher was about to say something important. Students gathered around to listen. In Matthew 5, the "Sermon on the Mount," Jesus sat down to talk with his disciples. The disciples gathered around him. Jesus looked up at those he was teaching.

Lesson 10: Who is Jesus?

One way we can get to know Jesus is by studying his teachings and observing what he did. We will do this now by observing Jesus as he teaches his disciples. Let's enter this story together. One member of your team will read the Sermon on the Mount from Luke 6:17–49. The reader should sit in a lower place and the listeners should gather around. Listen as if you were in the original audience, hearing Jesus' message for the first time. Take notes on the following questions:

- What do you learn about Jesus' character from his actions and his teaching?

- What does Jesus value? How do you know?

- What does Jesus expect from those who follow him?

Discuss your answers as a team. Note any common themes in your answers.

 Application

With your answers to the previous questions in mind, think about your own life.

- Think about the instructions that Jesus gives in Luke 6:27–38. How well do you measure up? In Luke 6:43–45, Jesus mentions the fruit that will be evident in "good trees." What fruit do you see in your life?

- Describe the foundation of your life. How do you know it is what you think it is?

Share your self-reflections in groups of two or three. At the end, pray for each other in your small group.

✝ Prayer

In your large group, identify several favorite songs or hymns about Jesus and sing them together as a prayer.

Digging Deeper

Pray and ask Jesus to show you one area of your life in which you could be more like him. As you go about your ministry experience, look for opportunities to develop in this area.

More Resources
- Josh McDowell. *More Than a Carpenter.* New York: Phoenix Press, 1986.
- Michael J. Wilkins and J. P. Moreland, eds. *Jesus Under Fire: Modern Scholarship Reinvents the Historical Jesus.* Grand Rapids, Mich.: Zondervan Publishing House, 1995.
- Philip Yancey. *The Jesus I Never Knew.* Grand Rapids, Mich.: Zondervan Publishing House, 1995.

Lesson 11
What is discipleship?

Jesus went out again beside the sea;
the whole crowd gathered around him, and he taught them.
As he was walking along, he saw Levi son of Alphaeus
sitting at the tax booth, and he said to him,
"Follow me." And he got up and followed him.
—Mark 2:13–14

➡ Starter

Think about something you have learned to do (for example, play an instrument, play a game, do an art activity, use a computer). How did you learn your new skill? Did you have a teacher? If so, how did that person help you learn? At what point did you (or will you) become a musician, an athlete, an artist, or a computer whiz? How do you know when you have "arrived?"

 Study

As Jesus began preparing to leave this world, he gave important instructions to the disciples about how they were to love one another after he was gone. Jesus' teaching involved both demonstration and direction. In John 13, Jesus uses the basin and the towel as symbols of his kind of discipleship. First, have one person read John 13:1–20 out loud. Then, identify three readers for this passage—a narrator, Jesus, and Simon Peter—and read it again.

- How did Jesus demonstrate his love for the disciples?

- How did they respond?

- What does Jesus teach about the relationship between teachers and students/disciples?

- What did Jesus call his disciples to do?

Application

Jesus instructed his disciples to follow his example. But foot washing is not a typical part of twenty-first century culture. What would be some examples of how you could "wash one another's feet" today in your group? In this city? Choose one example and do it.

Prayer

Antiphonal prayer is a way of praying back and forth between two people or two groups of people. Generate a list of things that you believe God is calling you to during this time of ministry. Have one person or group of people identify those things in prayer. As a response to each statement, say John 13:17 together: "If you know these things, you are blessed if you do them."

Digging Deeper

Although foot washing is not a typical part of our worship today, participating in a foot-washing service can be a significant experience. Doing something out of our ordinary experience can help us be open to God's voice. Plan a foot-washing service with your team. As you wash each other's feet, ask God to teach you how to follow the Spirit more closely. Ask the Lord to open your eyes to ways in which you can serve others.

More Resources
- Leroy Eims. *The Lost Art of Discipleship.* Grand Rapids, Mich.: Zondervan Book House, 1978.
- Alice Fryling. *Disciple-makers Handbook.* Downers Grove, Ill.: InterVarsity Press, 1989.
- Waylon B. Moore. *Multiplying Disciples: The New Testament Method for Church Growth.* Tampa, Fla.: Missions Unlimited, 1981.

Lesson 12
How should we pray?

After Jesus had spoken these words,
he looked up to heaven and said . . . .
—John 17:1

➔ Starter

Think about a significant, intimate conversation that you have had with someone important to you. In your group, discuss and then develop a list of the qualities, behaviors, or words that made the conversation meaningful.

📖 Study

Jesus is the model for our lives as Christians. By studying his life, we can discover ways in which we are to become like him. In John 17, Jesus prays for himself, his disciples, and for all believers. Study this passage as one model of how we should pray.

- Look through the passage and focus on the relationship that Jesus has with the Father. Using examples from the text, describe their relationship.

- Make a list of what Jesus prays for on behalf of himself, his disciples, all believers, and those in the world. What do Jesus' prayers reveal about his relationships with God and with others? about his hopes for them?

- Look again and notice the connection between Jesus' prayers and his actions. How would you describe the connection between what Jesus prays and what he does?

 ## Application

Think about your prayer life. Review the list that you developed of markers of intimate, significant conversation. Compare that list with your insights about Jesus' prayer in John 17.

- Which of those markers characterize your conversation with God?

- In what areas are you dissatisfied with your prayer relationship with God?

Discuss your answers with a partner.

 ## Prayer

Pray as Jesus did: for yourselves, your coworkers, other believers, and those in the world. What would Jesus have you pray for yourself? for one another? for the believers in the community in which you are serving? for the nonbelievers in the community? Take time to pray. Spend some time talking and some time listening. God might lead you to pray in certain ways, or God might respond to your requests.

 ## Digging Deeper

Jesus prayed that the believers would be brought to complete unity so that the world might know the reality of God's love and Christ's love for the world. What barriers to complete unity are you experiencing on your team? What can you do to overcome these barriers? Discuss these barriers to unity and then pray and ask God to guide you in overcoming them.

More Resources

- Arnold B. Cheyney. *Writing: A Way to Pray.* Chicago: Loyola University Press, 1995.
- Joyce Huggett. P*rayer: The Joy of Listening to God.* Downers Grove, Ill.: InterVarsity Press, 1986.
- Henri Nouwen. *The Way of the Heart.* New York: Ballantine Books, 1981.
- Richard Peace. *Spiritual Journaling.* Colorado Springs: NavPress, 1995.

Lesson 13
How can we develop spiritual disciplines?

Not that I have already obtained this
or have already reached the goal;
but I press on to make it my own,
because Christ Jesus has made me his own.
Beloved, I do not consider that I have made it my own;
but this one thing I do: forgetting what lies behind
and straining forward to what lies ahead,
I press on toward the goal for the prize
of the heavenly call of God in Christ Jesus.
—Philippians 3:12–14

➡) Starter

Think about a race or a contest in which you have participated. What was your strategy for participating in the race or contest? What was your goal? Did your strategy work? Develop a list of how the members of your group approach challenges such as races or contests. What does this tell you about your group?

📖 Study

Christians have practiced many spiritual disciplines throughout the ages in order to help people know and become more like God. Richard Foster, in his book *Streams of Living Water: Celebrating the Great Traditions of the Christian Faith*, describes six different streams in historic Christianity, each with its own spiritual emphases, strengths, and practices. The contemplative tradition is known for the prayer-filled life. Those in the holiness tradition focus on virtuous living. The charismatic tradition relies on the Spirit for empowerment. Those in the social justice tradition engage in acts of justice and compassion. The evangelical tradition is Word-centered. The incarnation tradition is known for the sacramental life. Each tradition practices "disciplines" that can help believers live lives that glorify God. Common to the appropriate practice of all these disciplines is a devotion to God and a desire to become more Christlike. How does this happen? Surely God has already been at work in your lives, so take some time to learn from one another. Fill in the following chart. One list is of disciplines that you have practiced effectively and that helped you to grow closer to God. The other list is of disciplines either that you tried to practice and couldn't follow through or that you did practice, but they didn't seem to have any life in them. First, fill in the row about your life.

	Disciplines that helped me get closer to God	Disciplines that seemed ineffective
My life		
Other group members' answers		

Next, share your answers with the group, and record their answers on your chart. Review the two lists, considering the following questions.

- Are there disciplines that appear on both lists? If so, what made them effective for one person and not effective for another?

- Evaluate the disciplines that appear on your lists. Are they primarily individual or corporate disciplines?

- Are there strategies for practicing the disciplines that are common on the list of effective disciplines?

- What barriers do you identify on your lists to practicing disciplines effectively?

Application

Review the "Personal and Corporate Disciplines" list in Appendix F. Choose a partner and together identify one new discipline and practice it during the next week. Talk specifically about what you will do, when you will practice the discipline, where you will practice, what you hope to learn, and with whom you will practice (if it is a corporate discipline). At the end of the week, discuss what happened.

✝ Prayer

Choose a hymn and sing it together as a prayer.

 Digging Deeper

Although putting effort into our discipleship is important, it is also important to remember that our effort is not sufficient to accomplish God's work. In some cases, lack of success could be the result of spiritual warfare. Ephesians 6:12 reminds us that we wrestle not against flesh and blood, but against principalities and powers. Individually review the full armor of God that is listed in Ephesians 6:13–20 using the following chart. Discuss with your team how you might be more intentional about wearing God's armor.

Lesson 13: How can we develop spiritual disciplines?

Piece of armor	How this piece of armor works	Purpose for this piece of armor	How well am I utilizing this piece of armor

More Resources

- Richard J. Foster. *Celebration of Discipline: The Path to Spiritual Growth.* 3rd ed. San Francisco: HarperSanFrancisco, 1988.
- ——. *Freedom of Simplicity.* San Francisco: Harper & Row, 1981.
- ——. *Streams of Living Water: Celebrating the Great Traditions of the Christian Faith.* San Francisco: HarperSanFrancisco, 1998.
- Bob Morley. *Aerobics for the Spirit.* Dallas: Word Publishing, 1990.
- Dallas Willard. *The Spirit of the Disciplines: Understanding How God Changes Lives.* San Francisco: HarperSanFrancisco, 1988.

Lesson 14
How is God shaping people for ministry?

[Mordecai] sent back this answer:
"Do not think that because you are in the king's house
you alone of all the Jews will escape. For if you remain silent at
this time, relief and deliverance for the Jews will arise from
another place, but you and your father's family will perish.
And who knows but that you have come
to royal position for such a time as this?"
Then Esther sent this reply to Mordecai:
"Go, gather together all the Jews who are in Susa,
and fast for me. Do not eat or drink for three days, night or day.
I and my maids will fast as you do. When this is done,
I will go to the king, even though it is against the law.
And if I perish, I perish."
—Esther 4:13–16, NIV

→ Starter

Think about someone you know who has made a difference in the world. What draws your interest to this person? What unique qualities or abilities or attributes shaped that individual for what he or she has accomplished? In the space below, make a list of the qualities identified by members of your group.

📖 Study

God knew each one of us when we were being formed and intended that we would come to know, love, and serve our Creator. The Lord invites each one of us to use our uniqueness for divine purposes. Rick Warren, author of *The Purpose Driven Church*, uses the acronym SHAPES to describe how God prepares people to be disciples in the world. We have modified this acronym and the concepts to which it refers and will give a very brief summary description of each aspect of SHAPES. We invite you to continue to explore these ideas through prayer, conversation, journaling and reflection—even after you finish this urban experience. Read through the following descriptions out loud and then discuss the ideas. Ask how these insights can help you to understand yourselves and each other more fully.

S • God gives each person at least one **spiritual gift.** That gift or those gifts influence the way in which a person is able to love and serve God and others. Gifts are given to an individual on behalf of the church and are to be used to build God's kingdom, not for personal gain. The biblical story of the multiplication of the loaves and fishes is a good illustration of how that which is offered to God multiplies in order to meet the needs of others.

H • Our **heart's passion** or what we love influences the choices we make, the directions we choose, and our motivations for doing what we do. You can tell a lot about a person by what he or she loves. Scripture reminds us that where our treasure is, our hearts will be also. Identifying what you really love provides the basis for understanding how your passions line up with what God loves.

A • In addition to spiritual gifts, we have natural **abilities, aptitudes,** and **attitudes.** A person may have the capacity or aptitude to develop new abilities throughout life. When natural abilities are used and maximized, we are motivated, energized, and feel satisfied and full. We are motivated to use some abilities more than others and have a positive attitude towards those abilities. When our abilities are dormant or neglected, we can experience a sense of emptiness or a feeling that something is missing from life. When people do work that depends on weaknesses instead of strengths, they often feel frustrated or uncomfortable. Recognizing your natural abilities and aptitudes will help you to make choices that are consistent with your design.

P • Each person has a distinctive **personality** that influences how he or she relates to other people, gathers information, and approaches tasks. There are numerous instruments and models that explore and describe unique personalities. Understanding your own personality and the existence of other ways of being in the world is a first step in promoting effective communication and healthy interpersonal relationships.

E • The life **experiences** that make up each person's story (for example, experiences of brokenness or wholeness, times of economic blessings or difficulties, types of education or miseducation) impact what each individual has to give. Sharing our stories with each other provides a window into other aspects of how we have been shaped by God. Both our victories and our difficulties help us to become more like God and to minister to the world.

S • In addition, a person's **season in life** will influence the ministry options, personal obligations, and available time for service. Recognizing the benefits and liabilities of your season in life and living with them as parameters will help to reduce frustration and to clarify opportunities that God may be presenting during a particular season. For example, a young single adult generally has more schedule flexibility than a parent of five young children. But, the young single adult and the parent of the children each will have unique relationships and unique options for ministry that someone in a different season in life will not have.

God shapes us in and through these aspects of life. Like the unique shape of a puzzle piece, our "shape" makes us a better fit for some ministry situations than others. As we learn to identify how God shapes us, we can be more receptive to the ways in which we are called to follow God's lead.

 Application

God has given you a great resource in your team members. Begin by taking no more than two minutes per person to share one significant life event that reveals something about who God has created you to be. Then, if you have time, explore each other's life stories in more detail. Listen for how God shapes each person.

 Prayer

Rejoice in the special way God has shaped each person on your team. Take time to thank God for each person individually and for the unique shape that he or she brings to your group. Ask the Lord to show you how you can encourage one another and work together most effectively as a team.

 Digging Deeper

The story of Esther provides a good starting point to begin identifying how God shapes people for ministry. Purim is a traditional Jewish festival celebrating the story of Esther. Part of the celebration is that everyone participates in the retelling of this story. To help you to focus on the story, we invite you to participate as if you are a typical group celebrating Purim. Identify one person to retell the story found in the book of Esther. When the name of Haman is mentioned, the storyteller will give enough time for everyone in

Lesson 14: How is God shaping people for ministry?

SHAPES	Questions	Answers
Spiritual gifts	What spiritual gifts does Esther demonstrate?	
Heart passion	What does Esther love? How do we know? What is she willing to die for?	
Abilities, aptitudes, attitudes	What skills does Esther use to accomplish her goals?	
Personality	What behaviors do we see in Esther that give us a clue about her personality?	
Experiences in life	What events in Esther's life make her the unique person that she is? What experiences of brokenness does God use for good? What experiences of privilege enable her to minister effectively?	
Season in life	How did Esther's season in life influence her ability to make an impact in her world?	

the group to boo and hiss. Some people may bang pots and pans or use other noise makers. When Esther's name is mentioned, the group will call out "Blessed be Esther" in a loud, but reverent voice. After reading the story, think through the SHAPES questions on the chart and apply them to Esther.

After discussing the chart, conclude with the following questions.

- How does Esther's life encourage/discourage you?

- What difference did Esther make in the course of history?

- What insights do you gain about how God works in people's lives from the story of Esther?

Take several minutes to imagine you are one of the attendants in the story. (Imagine their words, their feelings, their physical postures, the flow of the prayer, their passion, etc.) How would you have prayed for Esther? Write down a few notes for yourself. Each person should identify for the group one thing about which he or she believes God is speaking to his or her heart. Pray for one person at a time. Pray for one another in the way you imagine the attendants would have prayed for Esther.

More Resources

- Os Guinness. *The Call: Finding and Fulfilling the Central Purpose of Your Life.* Nashville: Word Publishing, 1998.
- Donald P. McNeill, Douglas A. Morrison, Henri J. M. Nouwen. *Compassion: A Reflection on the Christian Life.* New York: Image Books, Doubleday, 1982.
- Les Steele. *On the Way: A Practical Theology of Christian Formation.* Grand Rapids, Mich.: Baker Book House, 1990.
- Rick Warren. *The Purpose Driven Church.* Grand Rapids, Mich.: Zondervan Press, 1995.

Lesson 15
How is God shaping me for ministry?

For as in one body we have many members,
and not all the members have the same function,
so we, who are many, are one body in Christ,
and individually we are members one of another.
We have gifts that differ according to the grace given to us:
prophecy, in proportion to faith; ministry, in ministering;
the teacher, in teaching; the exhorter, in exhortation;
the giver, in generosity; the leader, in diligence;
the compassionate, in cheerfulness.
—Romans 12:4–8

→ Starter

Choose a fruit or vegetable that somehow represents you and your SHAPES (see Lesson 14) or how God is shaping you for ministry. Introduce your fruit or vegetable and why it describes you.

 Study

The following activities are designed to help you articulate the ways in which God has been shaping you. The size and dynamics of the group, how much time you have, and what you are trying to accomplish will suggest to you which activities are most appropriate for your group. Consider using this lesson several times, using different activities each time.

Spiritual gifts

One person will read aloud the following lists of spiritual gifts: Romans 12:6–8, Ephesians 4:11–13, 1 Corinthians 12:1–11. The lists contain some common gifts and some discrete gifts; they probably do not provide us with an exhaustive list. These gifts are ones God has given to the church through individuals. There could be other gifts that aren't mentioned. As you listen to these passages, think about how you have been involved in kingdom work. You may identify some of your gifts by thinking about what you actually do and what types of activities energize you. But, you also may have gifts that you haven't used or discovered yet, so don't be too conclusive in your decision. Ask yourself:

- How has God used me to minister to others?

- What gifts do people tell me they see in my life?

Take turns telling the group about the gifts that you think God might have entrusted to you. Listen carefully. Affirm the gifts that you see evident in the speaker's life.

Heart passion

Divide into groups of two or three. Answer the following questions, one person at a time. Practice really listening to one another. Take turns summarizing what you have heard from one of the speakers about what he or she really loves.

- When you have free time, how do you spend it?

- What would you be willing to die for?

- What are you passionate about? What do you love?

- What concerns has God placed on your heart? What draws you?

- What do you love that God loves? What do you love that God is not pleased about?

Abilities, aptitudes, and attitudes

Have one person at a time sit outside the group circle with his or her back to the group. The group will engage in positive gossip about this person as if he or she weren't there. The person being talked about cannot respond, but only listen. The following questions will help you think about each person's abilities. Have one person in the group record the positive feedback for the listener.

- What skills does this person have?

Lesson 15: How is God shaping me for ministry?

- What does this person do well?

- What seems to motivate this person?

- What is this person's most valuable personal asset?

- How have you seen God using this person's abilities for the kingdom?

Personality

This activity is designed to help you think about a few of your preferences for life and how your group as a whole fits on these dimensions. As a group, you will order yourselves on several continuums to reflect where each person fits in relationship to the others in the group. Identify two points on either side of the room to serve as an "anchor" point for the extreme ends. First, think about where you fit on the continuum. Then try to fit yourself in with the other members of the group. You will need to ask each other some questions to see how strong your preferences are compared with theirs. Remember, these continuums are preferences. Some people will have stronger preferences than others. There are no "right" answers or ways to be. The preferences chosen here are based on the Meyers/Briggs Type Indicator, but there are many other instruments that you could use to explore personal preferences or personality strengths. (If you want to look more closely into the Meyers/Briggs Type Indicator, see *Please Understand Me,* by David Keirsey and Marilyn Bates.)

- Do you get energy from:
  within yourself . . . . **being with others**

- Do you get information from:
  what could be/ . . . . **what exists/what you**
  possibilities   **perceive with your senses**

- Do you make decisions based on:
  what is right . . . . **how the decision will**
  influence people

- Do you like to:
  keep your options open . . . . **have closure and completeness**

Lesson 15: How is God shaping me for ministry?

Experiences in life

This exercise will help your group to reflect on your life stories. Use a big sheet of paper and make a timeline that identifies five-year periods of time (e.g., 0–5, 6–10, 11–15 etc.). Include enough periods to account for the oldest member of your group. Have each person choose a different color marker or crayon and identify a significant life event during as many time periods as possible. Think about stories of success and failure, times of well-being and woundedness, your history with God and the church, significant relationships and any other life events that come to mind and develop a symbol to indicate what you want to remember. If there is a particular event that is too personal to share, but has had an important influence on you, indicate that event with the letters "PE" (personal event). When the time line is finished, take turns sharing some of the significant stories behind the symbols with the group. Then, review the patterns you see on the whole group's time line.

- Are there periods of time that have been particularly influential for your group?

- What common themes do you see among your group members?

- What unique ways has God used situations in the lives of individuals in this group?

- What implication do the patterns (or lack of patterns) have for this group and what you have to offer to others?

Season in life

Think about your season in life. Think about the different components of your season in life, for example your age, roles, responsibilities, relationships, and affiliations (e.g., single, married, parent, student, missionary, second-career, searching, sister, church member etc.). Make a pie chart in which you divide the pie into variously sized pieces that represent how each of the different components of your life fit together. Share your pies with one another, either in pairs or all together. As a large group, brainstorm the benefits of the season of each person's life. Think about issues such as available time, energy, responsibilities, options, etc.

✎ Application

Journal about what you learned about yourself in these exercises.

- How has your unique SHAPES prepared you for this urban ministry adventure?

- What do you bring to the group that is needed?

- What are your limits or weaknesses?

- What do you not have that you need other members of the group to bring?

Share significant insights with the group.

Lesson 15: How is God shaping me for ministry?

✚ Prayer

This time of prayer is based on the ACTS acronym—Adoration, Confession, Thanksgiving, and Supplication.

- Begin with a time of adoration of God and the image of God present in each team member. Thank God for the gifts, abilities, aptitudes, passions, and personalities of each one and how these qualities are a reflection of God's character.

- Confess any ways that you have not been a good steward of the person God has made you to be.

- Thank God for the benefits made available to you during this season in life and for God's help in making the most of those benefits.

- Ask God to help you to be a good steward of all the gifts and resources made available to the church through you.

🧠 Digging Deeper

Option one is to write your own obituary. For what do you want to be remembered? What do you want to accomplish in your life? Option two is to write a eulogy for someone else in the group based on what you learned about him or her from this activity. Read your obituary or eulogy out loud to the group. Listen to those read by others and remember these insights about your team.

More Resources

- Margaret Guenther. *Holy Listening: The Art of Spiritual Direction.* Cambridge, Mass.: Cowley Publication, 1992.
- David Keirsey and Marilyn Bates. *Please Understand Me.* Delmar, Calif.: Prometheus Nemesis Book Company, 1984.

Lesson 16
How do we share the gospel?

But you will receive power
when the Holy Spirit has come upon you;
and you will be my witnesses in Jerusalem,
in all Judea and Samaria, and to the ends of the earth.
—Acts 1:8

 **Starter**

Brainstorm together a list of ways to share the gospel. It may include specific methods, Scriptures, or more general types of conversation or behavior. Go around the group and list your ideas. Write your ideas on the diagram below. Notice any trends or themes.

Content approach   **Relational approach**
Word-centered   **People-centered**
(e.g., Roman Road,   (e.g., friendship
Four Spiritual Laws)   evangelism)

Lesson 16: How do we share the gospel?

📖 Study

Begin developing an approach to sharing the gospel by remembering how others shared the gospel with you. With a partner, spend ten minutes discussing your own spiritual development. What or who helped you grow spiritually? How were the "basics" of the faith introduced to you? Were there any people, methods, books, or situations that harmed your understanding of God or the gospel? Discuss your reflections with your team. Do you see themes among your team members of effective or ineffective ministry strategies?

How did Jesus share the good news of God's kingdom with his disciples? Use your Bible as needed to answer the following questions. Use the Gospels as a resource to refresh your memory about how Jesus approached discipleship and evangelism. You may want to divide into four groups and have each group use one of the Gospels as a reference to guide its thinking.

- How did Jesus spend time with his disciples? How much time did he spend with them?

- What kind of relationships did Jesus form with his disciples?

- How did Jesus help develop his disciples' faith?

- Read John 15:9–16. How did Jesus feel about his disciples?

- As you go out to make disciples in the city, what does Jesus' example teach you?

Application

As a team, having a common vision for sharing the gospel will help you as you seek to minister to others. Although you may each use different Scripture verses, styles, or approaches that make you comfortable, it's okay to be yourself and share with people in your own way. Take time to write down the approaches toward sharing the Good News that your group has in common. What is essential in sharing the gospel and making disciples? What is essential for your group, in this city?

 Prayer

Spend a few moments in silence, reflecting on Jesus' command to you to share the gospel with others. Pray sentence prayers about your personal involvement in the spreading of the gospel. Bring your thanks, your memories, and your fears before the Lord in prayer.

 **Digging Deeper**

Role play a situation in which you may share your faith. Think of a realistic situation for your group. It may be sharing the gospel for the first time, or it may be discipling a new Christian in the faith. Two or three people will act out a scene. Afterwards, the entire group will encourage and evaluate the role play. What parts of the role play are useful for your group as you minister in the city? What parts are not very helpful?

More Resources

- Robert G. Duffett. *A Relevant Word: Communicating the Gospel to Seekers.* Valley Forge, Pa.: Judson Press, 1995.
- Duncan McIntosh. *The Everyday Evangelist.* Valley Forge, Pa.: Judson Press, 1984.
- Jim Petersen. *Living Proof: Sharing the Gospel Naturally.* Colorado Springs: NavPress, 1989.
- William L. Turner. *Anytime, Anywhere: Sharing Faith Jesus Style.* Valley Forge, Pa.: Judson Press, 1997.

unit four

Building Community Together

Lesson 17
What can we expect in community?

And let us consider how to provoke one another to love
and good deeds, not neglecting to meet together,
as is the habit of some, but encouraging one another,
and all the more as you see the Day approaching.
—*Hebrews 10:24–25*

➜ Starter

As a group, discuss how you view yourselves.

- Are you a "group"? a "team"? a "community"? or something else?

- What determined your choice of a label?

- What does your choice say about who you are, and who you want to be?

You may not reach consensus in the time allotted for this activity, and that's fine. Close the discussion, acknowledging the variety of ideas, and move on.

📖 Study

Shortly after Jesus' death and resurrection, the followers of Christ had to make decisions about their "group." Who were they? What did they have in common? How would they live? On the day of Pentecost, described in Acts 2, the believers experienced the Holy Spirit in a powerful way, and began to live together in a new way. Their example can provide encouragement and inspiration to us today as we follow Christ together. Read Acts 2 out loud, reflecting and taking notes on the following questions.

● How did these Christians experience the Holy Spirit?

● How did these believers live?

● How would you describe their form of community?

● What form of community does your group currently have (shared commitments or values, resources, time, etc.)?

Application

One important part of a community, team, or group situation is knowing one's own expectations, others' expectations, and the shared consensus of the group. No group is all things to all its members, but by making expectations spoken and known, your group can grow in directions appreciated by all. Individuals with significant differences may choose to change their expectations, help change the group's expectations, or decide they need to find a different group.

Spend a few minutes thinking about your expectations for this group. Write answers to the following questions.

● Imagine this group at its very best. What words would describe it?

● What do you want to offer this group? (Time, money, intimacy, encouragement, energy, friendship, etc.)

- What would you like to get from this group?

- Do you expect conflicts in your group? Are there any benefits that may come from conflict?

Prepare yourself to share with the group, and to listen to other members share their hopes and expectations. Listen for similarities and differences. When everyone has shared, talk about what you heard. Did you hear similar ideas about what this group might become? Did you hear significant differences?

 **Prayer**

Begin by reading your answers to the question, "What words would describe this group at its very best?" Ask God to help you bring those words to life in your group.

Digging Deeper

Reflect on what the lifestyle of the early church could mean for your group. How far could you go in pursuing unity and community? What risks might you take? Don't worry about practicalities; rather, use this time for dreaming together about what your group could become.

More Resources

- Dietrich Bonhoeffer. *Life Together: A Discussion of Christian Fellowship.* San Francisco: HarperSanFrancisco, 1992.
- Joan Chittister. *Wisdom Distilled From the Daily: Living the Rule of St. Benedict Today.* San Francisco: Harper & Row, 1990.
- Henri Nouwen. *The Genessee Diary: Report from a Trappist Monastery.* New York: Doubleday, 1976.

Lesson 18

How can we partner with God's people in this city?

There is no longer Jew or Greek,
there is no longer slave or free,
there is no longer male and female;
for all of you are one in Christ Jesus.
—Galatians 3:28

 **Starter**

Think about the best experience you've had at a church. Share it with the group. What made it so good? Listen for common themes between stories.

 **Study**

This study is designed to help you think about divisions between Christians today, and how your group can promote unity. American churches often function independently, or in cooperation with churches most like themselves. Churches rarely partner across social boundaries of geography (urban, rural, suburban), class (rich, poor, working class, middle class), race, culture, ethnicity, or language. Divisions between American churches often reflect and perpetuate social divisions in American society.

Let's start by looking at a different situation in the early church, a situation in which Peter learned to see the gospel in a new way. In the time of the early church, social boundaries between Jews and Gentiles were very significant, and those prejudices and divisions continued in the church between believers of Jewish and Gentile cultural backgrounds. In this story, Peter (a Jewish Christian) and Cornelius (a Gentile Christian) have an encounter that transforms Peter's understanding of the faith. He describes what he learned to other Jewish believers in chapter 11 of Acts.

Read Acts 10:1–11:18 together, going around the group as each person reads several verses. Then, have one or two people tell the story in their own words. Make sure that each person in your group has a clear understanding of the narrative. Take notes on key characters and events.

Lesson 18: How can we partner with God's people in this city?

Reflect on the following questions as you read and listen. Then discuss them afterward.

• What did Peter learn from the vision of the sheet and animals?

• What made it so hard for Peter to respond to and act on his vision?

• What are the main ideas in Peter's speech (Acts 10:34–43)? How might these ideas have challenged the original audience? How do these ideas challenge you?

Application

Urban ministry means more than "bringing the gospel" to people who have never heard it. In urban America, thousands of Christians and churches are already following Christ and sharing the gospel in their neighborhoods. Sometimes the social divisions between churches (geography, class, race, and culture) make it hard for new urban ministers to see the presence of Christ already in the city. Sometimes "urban ministry" means repairing those breaches between believers both before and while we share the gospel with nonbelievers.

Discuss the following questions and then retell the story of Acts 10 in your current context.

• Instead of Jewish Christians and Gentile Christians, what are current groups of Christians that are separated by social or cultural divisions?

• Instead of circumcision and food taboos, what are some of the issues (worship styles, language, cultural practices, etc.) that separate American Christians?

- How could your group be proactive about addressing divisions between Christians in your area? Be as specific as possible.

- How could this work between believers build your capacity to share the gospel with nonbelievers?

 **Prayer**

As a group, read John 17:20–21. Pray together for unity among believers. Pray specifically for the American church, naming its divisions and asking the Holy Spirit to help your group become proactive promoters of unity in your county, suburb, or city.

Digging Deeper

Think of two practical ways that you can partner with God's people who are already working in the city. This may mean building relationships or partnerships with churches you already know, or it may mean introducing yourselves to Christians in the area where you plan to work. Appendix E is a guide to observing and experiencing worship in an unfamiliar tradition.

More Resources

- Daniel L. Buttry. *Christian Peacemaking: From Heritage to Hope.* Valley Forge, Pa.: Judson Press, 1994.
- ——. *Peace Ministry: A Handbook for Local Churches.* Valley Forge, Pa.: Judson Press, 1995.
- Susan D. Newman. *With Heart and Hand: The Black Church Working to Save Black Children.* Valley Forge, Pa.: Judson Press, 1994.

Lesson 19
How can we resolve our conflicts?

Then Peter came and said to [Jesus],
"Lord, if another member of the church sins against me,
how often should I forgive? As many as seven times?"
Jesus said to him, "Not seven times, but, I tell you, seventy-seven times."
—*Matthew 18:21*

➜ Starter

Sit in a circle. Choose a timekeeper. For one minute, focus on one person in the group. Speak affirming words to that person about the way he or she functions as a group member. Only affirmations are allowed! The person on the "hot seat" may not speak other than to say "thanks." Move through the group, being sure that each person is included.

📖 Study

In the Bible, Jesus and Paul have much to say about conflicts between believers. They expect it! Working through conflicts in a healthy way can bring a relationship to a new level of integrity and intimacy. We encourage you to anticipate conflicts in your group. Use this study to discuss ways of handling conflict, even before it occurs. Resolving conflict successfully will enable your group to stay together, and stay close, for the long haul.

Read Matthew 18:15–20 out loud. Discuss the following questions in pairs, and then as an entire group.

- If Matthew 18 were a newspaper article, what would the headline be?

- What is the responsibility of the person who is offended?

- What is the responsibility of the person who is being confronted?

- What is the responsibility of other believers, who may have no immediate involvement in the conflict?

 Application

As a group, discuss the following questions.

- Have you ever seen or experienced a conflict that was resolved in the way described in Matthew 18:15–20? What might these principles mean for your group?

- When conflict occurs, what are the responsibilities of the people involved? What is the group's responsibility?

- Do you have typical ways of dealing with conflict? Do you want to continue this approach, or are you working to change? Share with the group. "When I'm in conflict, I usually . . . ."

✝ Prayer

Pray silently for a few minutes, focusing on your personal strengths and weaknesses in conflict. Then pray out loud together, asking God to help your team build unity and strength through healthy conflict resolution.

🗣 Digging Deeper

As a group, develop a conflict resolution covenant. Develop a shared approach to conflicts when they arise. "When we are in conflict with each other, we will. . . ." It can be very specific, or it can focus on principles that you all value. Some helpful Scriptures may include Matthew 7:1–5; 18:15–20; 18:21–35; Ephesians 4:25–27; James 3:13–18.

More Resources

- G. Brian Jones and Linda Phillips-Jones. *A Fight to the Better End.* Wheaton, Ill.: Victor Books, 1989.
- M. Scott Peck. *A Different Drum.* New York: Simon & Schuster, 1987.
- Ken Sande. *The Peacemaker: A Biblical Guide to Resolving Personal Conflict.* Grand Rapids, Mich.: Baker Books, 1991.

Lesson 20
How are we doing?

*But speaking the truth in love, we must grow up in every way
into him who is the head, into Christ, from whom the whole
body, joined and knit together by every ligament with which it
is equipped, as each part is working properly, promotes the
body's growth in building itself up in love.*
—Ephesians 4:15–16

 Starter

Think about how well your group is working together to promote each other's spiritual
formation, to begin urban ministry, to learn about your city, and to become a unified
community of believers. Imagine you are taking your group's temperature. On a scale of
one to ten, where would you place the group? One is the low end, meaning that the group
has very serious problems. Ten is the high end, meaning the group is functioning at a high
level of health. Go around the circle and state your numbers, with very brief comments.
Use this exercise to get a sense for how members see the group. More detailed discussion
will come during the study and application sections.

 Study

Ask yourselves, "How are we doing?" This is not a time for confronting individuals or for
evaluating yourself as an individual, although this discussion may reveal a need for that.
Think of yourselves as the body of Christ, working together to minister to each other and
in the city.

Evaluate actions and attitudes regarding the following issues. Add issues if others are
important. Identify the one area where you feel the group is strongest, and mark it with
a plus (+). Identify the area where you feel the group is weakest, and give that area a
minus (−).

    ____ **preparing for meetings**
    ____ **participating in meetings**
    ____ **learning about the city**

_____ building partnerships in the city

_____ praying

_____ interpersonal relationships within the group

_____ addressing and resolving conflict

_____ communicating respectfully and honestly

_____ demonstrating a servant's heart toward serving others

_____ being on time

_____ other: _____

_____ other: _____

_____ other: _____

Give each person an opportunity to identify an area of strength. Then discuss the weaknesses the group has identified. Different individuals will probably see different strengths and weaknesses, and what one person sees as the group's greatest strength may appear as a weakness to another person. What do you make of the strengths and weaknesses chosen by your group? Does this exercise raise any questions, concerns, or praises for you as a group? If so, what are they?

 ## Application

Develop specific steps for preserving and improving a strength or for improving a weakness. Identify one or two specific goals that your group can pursue over the next several weeks. Keep your goals SMART! Remember, SMART goals are Specific, Measurable, Actionable, Realistic, and Time-limited. For example, a group may want to focus on timeliness for meetings.

	SMART goals	Not-so-SMART goals
Specific	Come to meetings on time	Be more aware of time
Measurable	"On time" means within 5 minutes of our start time	In general, try to be on time
Actionable	Be in the room, and stop talking when the facilitator speaks	Always be ready to start
Realistic	We may need to make exceptions	No exceptions, ever!
Time-limited	For the next 4 meetings	For the rest of our group's time together

Your group's SMART goals:

1.

2.

 **Prayer**

Spend time thanking God for your group's strengths. Ask God to help you with your weaknesses, praying specifically about the goals you set.

Digging Deeper

Find a place in the room or building where each person has some private space. Reflect and write about the following questions. What were some important expectations you had for this group? Are they being met, or do they remain unmet? Come back together as a group and discuss your personal assessment of the group.

More Resources

- Dan Allender and Tremper Longman III. *Bold Love.* Colorado Springs: NavPress, 1992.
- Henry Cloud and John Townsend. *Boundaries: When to Say Yes, When to Say No To Take Control of Your Life.* Grand Rapids, Mich.: Zondervan, 1992.
- Stanley Grenz. *Created for Community: Connecting Christian Belief with Christian Living.* Grand Rapids, Mich.: Baker Books, 1998.

Lesson 21
How do we celebrate?!

What should be done then, my friends?
When you come together, each one has a hymn, a lesson,
a revelation, a tongue, or an interpretation.
Let all things be done for building up.
—1 Corinthians 14:26

➜ Starter

Celebrations are important for our own sakes, and also for those who join with us to celebrate. Think of the many celebrations in our lives—birthdays, weddings, graduations, baby showers, and others. Celebrations help us make memories that nourish and encourage us later on. They also serve as markers to help us recognize times of growth and change. We encourage your group to set aside time for celebration—of your hard work, of God's presence among you, of what you've learned, and of what you've received and given in ministry. Begin to celebrate by sharing ways in which God has spoken to you so far (through the city, new people you have met, group members, ministry you've participated in, etc.).

📖 Study

Think about what you've learned in this city so far. How have you seen people celebrate? Have you seen dances, parties, barbecues, birthdays, showers, weddings, etc.? Think of specific aspects of urban celebrations that you would like to incorporate into your life, or into the life of your group. If possible, choose one new celebratory activity that you will try out as a group.

Application

Spend time at this meeting in celebration! Choose an activity that suits your context and the interests of your group members. Suggestions:

- Go for a walk in the city. Look for your favorite parts of the city and talk about them.

- Celebrate specific accomplishments that your group has achieved. Discuss favorite memories, milestones, and people or situations that helped you achieve your goals.

- Celebrate the contributions of individual group members. Honor them with spoken or written words.

- Share new music or food that you have discovered in this city.

- As a group, create a visual memory of your time in the city.

Prayer

Choose a song that you have learned in the city to sing as joyful prayer and praise, affirming God's work in you and in this place. Choose other favorite hymns or choruses and sing them together.

Digging Deeper

As a group, plan a celebration that will include your new friends and coworkers in the urban community where you're working. It could be a breakfast or a dinner, held at a restaurant or someone's home . . . be creative! Celebrate what you've learned together about partnerships and about the city.

More Resources

- Tony Campolo. *The Kingdom of God Is a Party.* Dallas: Word Publishers, 1990.
- Diane C. Kessler. *God's Simple Gift: Meditations on Friendship and Spirituality.* Valley Forge, Pa.: Judson Press, 1988.

unit five

Endings

Lesson 22
What have we learned?

But may all who seek you
rejoice and be glad in you;
may those who love your salvation say continually,
"Great is the Lord!"
—Psalm 40:16

➔ Starter

Think back to your group's first meeting together or to the time when you first started this urban ministry venture. Review your journal entries. Tell stories of how your perceptions of the city, or of ministry, have changed. What were your initial impressions? Which impressions were proven true and which were false?

📓 Study

This exercise will help you assess your learning in several different areas, considering what you've learned about God, the city, yourselves, and your group. Complete the chart on page 77 by yourself, and then talk together as a group about what you learned. Look for similarities and differences in individual's answers, and see if a common picture emerges of what the group as a whole has learned.

Lesson 22: What have we learned?

Area of learning	What I/we have learned	Areas for more learning
About God		
About this city and urban ministry		
About myself and my faith		
About our group		

Application

Discuss what you wrote in the "Areas for more learning" column. Are there common themes that indicate a future direction for your group? Choose two or three areas for learning that are especially important to the group. Develop a strategy for investigating these areas over the next several weeks or months.

 Prayer

Arrange yourselves in a circle, and pray around the circle. Go around once, thanking God for specific things you've learned. Go around a second time, asking God for help in learning more about specific areas your group discussed. Any individual may say "Amen" to pass his or her turn to the next person.

Digging Deeper

Look over your personal or group "archives" of this experience. Archives include articles, letters, journals, and group records. Read them over, looking for situations, people, or learning moments you may have forgotten. Add them to your chart.

More Resources

- Ronald Klug. *How to Keep a Spiritual Journal.* Minneapolis: Augsburg Press, 1993.
- Richard Peace. *Spiritual Journaling.* Colorado Springs: NavPress, 1995.

Lesson 23
How do we make transitions?

For everything there is a season,
and a time for every matter under heaven.
—*Ecclesiastes 3:1*

 **Starter**

Tell the group how you typically leave a party. Do you try to slip out unnoticed? Do you make sure to say good-bye to everyone? Do you make plans to see people again? Often the way you will leave a party is typical of the way you deal with other transitions in your life. Is this true for you?

Study

This urban mission experience is coming to a close. It is time to think about how to take the things you have learned back home. How can you share your experience with others? How can you make sure you don't forget the lessons you have learned? A good beginning is to think about the process of transition itself and to identify strategies for coping with this particular transition.

A fundamental characteristic of transitions is change. Whether the change is happening for a positive reason (e.g., getting married, starting a new job, graduating, finishing this mission experience) or a negative reason (e.g., losing a job, losing a relationship), every transition has four predictable stages.

- The first stage in the process involves life before the transition. Life is generally known and understood.

- The second stage involves a death or an ending to the way things had been. For example, when you finish school and graduate, you have to say good-bye to life as a student and to all the benefits and the intensity of the relationships that exist in that environment. When someone gets married, there is a death to singleness and the benefits that go with being single.

- After the ending, there is an in-between time that has been called "the neutral zone." The old way of being is gone, but the new life has not yet been firmly established.

- The new beginning commences when you start feeling "at home" and "like yourself" again in the new place or in the "old" place with the "new" you. Understanding the predictable stages of transition will prepare you to deal with the emotions and the experiences inherent in the changes that happen in your life.

Review the chart, "The Characteristics of a Transition and Strategies for Coping," in Appendix G. Divide into four groups. Have each group study one of the stages, and then, using all the creativity you can muster, teach the other groups what you think they need to learn about your transition stage.

 Application

In your groups, explore the following questions. Then come back together and report common themes to the entire group.

- What has God done in our relationships as a team during this time together? What has God done through our work that we will be leaving behind?

- In what ways do I see things differently as a result of this urban ministry experience? How do I think this new ability to see will influence me back home? How do I feel about going home?

- What rituals or routines from this ministry opportunity do I want to incorporate into my life at home? What symbol or "artifact" can we bring home to remind us of God's work in this place?

- For what are we thankful?

✝ Prayer

Using again the format summarized by ACTS (adoration, confession, thanksgiving, supplication), take time to pray as a group for the upcoming transition that you will all be facing. Begin each phase of the prayer time with a reminder of what the focus will be, and read a Scripture that highlights that focus. For example:

- Adoration involves offering praise for the attributes and character of God, in other words, who God is (Psalm 99:1–5; 100).

- Confession is a time for us to confess to God the sins we have committed during this urban ministry experience and ask for mercy and forgiveness (Psalm 41:4; 1 John 1:9).

- Thanksgiving is a time to give thanks for the things God has done during this time of service and learning (Lamentations 3:22–23; Psalm 46:1–7).

- Supplication is a time for asking God for the things placed upon our hearts during this time set apart for service (Psalm 27:7–9; 28:2).

- A closing Scripture: Ephesians 3:20–21.

 **Digging Deeper**

Take time with one or two other people in your group to identify specific concerns you have about going back to your "regular" lives. Identify any potential pitfalls or temptations that you expect to face. Make a plan for accountability for the next three months.

More Resources

- Clyde N. Austin, ed. *Cross-Cultural Re-entry: A Book of Readings.* Abilene, Tx.: Abilene Christian University Press, 1986.
- William Bridges. *Transitions: Making Sense of Life's Changes.* Readings, Mass.: Addison-Wesley, 1980.
- Peter Jordan. *Re-Entry: Making the Transition from Missions to Life at Home.* Seattle: YWAM Publishing, 1992.

Lesson 24
How do we share what we've learned?

. . . "Great is the Lord,
who delights in the welfare of his servant."
Then my tongue shall tell of your righteousness
and of your praise all day long.
—Psalm 35:27–28

 Starter

Think of a single word that describes your urban ministry experience. Only one word! Go around the circle, sharing your words and a brief description. Write down other people's words if you think they capture your experience.

 Study

Spend some time alone working on the following questions. Then find a partner and discuss your answers.

- Think about who you want to share your experience with when you return home, or when the project ends. Be sure to remember people and organizations who have supported you with finances or prayer.

- List important artifacts—photos, maps, clothes, momentos, songs—that you would like to share with people. Are there ways to share some of these artifacts (without giving them away!)? Brainstorm possibilities, such as making a photo album, creating a recording, or developing a website or a computer slide presentation.

- Think about what you learned about your city—its streets, economy, architecture, assets, problems, people, neighborhoods, and churches. Brainstorm ways to share this kind of information, such as creating a map to share, or making a collection of key photos.

 Application

A common frustration experienced by many missionaries who come home and want to share their rich and complex experience with friends and supporters is that many people back home don't seem to be willing to take the time to listen. Hopefully you have a few people in your life with whom you can spend hours talking about what you saw and did, and how you changed. But, for those other people who don't have hours to spend, it is worth taking a few minutes to prepare for the many, briefer conversations that are likely to come.

- Imagine a friend of your parents stops you during coffee hour at church and says, "Good to see you! What did you do in the city?" She appears only to want to chat for a minute. Can you describe your experience in a minute or less? Spend time with a partner, condensing your experience into a sixty-second "blurb." There may be someone else who stops by after your parents' friend. This person seems to have a little more time and interest. Can you prepare a five-minute response to the same question?

- It may also be important to share what has happened during your ministry project with the people to whom God introduced you in the city. Think of key friends, neighbors, leaders, church members, or others who showed a special interest in your work, or in your personal development. Identify a way to talk with them about your experience before you leave. A corporate celebration, such as a potluck or sharing time, or a simple individual interaction, such as eating a meal together, taking a walk, or enjoying a phone conversation, are ways that you can remember how God worked in your lives through this urban adventure.

 Prayer

Practice intercessory prayer for the important people in your lives. Name the people with whom you plan to talk about your experience. Ask God to help them to truly listen and to learn more about God, you, your team, and the city.

 Digging Deeper

Talk with your group about how group members can stay in touch after the project ends. Groups sometimes develop creative ways to stay connected, sometimes for years after their experience together. An e-mail group, a website-based group, a phone prayer chain, and shared written letters are excellent ways to keep connected. Make a plan!

More Resources
- Leighton Ford. *The Power of Story.* Colorado Springs: NavPress, 1994.

appendixes

Appendix A
Journaling Suggestions

Why should you journal? Because journaling is an important spiritual discipline. The purpose of journaling is to establish patterns of intentional reflection in your life. Taking time to reflect and write can help you to grow in self-awareness, in your ability to speak and listen to God, and in your understanding of the Scriptures and your environment. Journaling can provide a space to work through conflict or questions. God may use your journaling to speak to you.

Make your journaling special. Get a notebook that is used only for journaling. Find a special place and time to journal, and use a good pen. You may want to begin your journaling with a daily record that lists what you did each day. A journal can become a memory bank of stories from the year, and the daily record can be a starting point for reflection. But not everyone writes every day. You should establish a pattern that is appropriate for you. The important thing to remember is to build a regular time and place in your schedule for reflection and writing.

The following list contains ideas for journaling. The lists are divided into categories that correspond with the workbook units. Sometimes it is helpful to begin with a question or idea. Other times, you may just write what is on your heart. Add your own journaling ideas for each unit.

Unit One: Beginnings
- What are your expectations and goals for this time in the city? What are some of your fears and hopes?
- What are your first impressions of my team? of this city?
- What did you see in the city today? What do you think of it? What might God think?
- What is your sense of place in the city? Do you belong? Do you feel like a visitor, a stranger, a friend, a neighbor? Do you want your sense of place to change, or are you comfortable with it the way it is?
-
-

Unit Two: Learning and Ministering in the City
- Write about a time when you helped someone. What happened? How did you know

what was needed? How do you know you helped them?

- Brainstorm a list of the words that you associate with "city." Write a prayer asking God to help you see the city the way God does.
- Write about the best urban experience you have had so far.
- What do you hope for? When have you experienced God's hope?
- Write about a success you've seen in the city.
- Use just one sense to experience the city. What do you see? smell? touch? taste? hear?
- Using a concordance, make a list of verses in the Bible that mention cities and reflect on one verse each day.
- Reflect on your church's or group's urban outreach efforts. What is working well? What isn't working?
- Write about something beautiful you saw in this city.
- Reflect on what you do in this city ministry. Are you growing in your faith? Are you developing skills?
-
-

Unit Three: Growing in Faith

- How are you feeling emotionally? Release those emotions in your journal. Set them before God before making decisions about handling them.
- How healthy are you? How do you care for your body?
- Write about family relationships. How have they nurtured you? How have they hurt you? Which patterns do you want to continue in your adult life? Which do you want to discontinue?
- Clarify your beliefs by choosing a word to write about: God, Jesus, Bible, prayer, Holy Spirit, mission, relationship, sin, justice, work, etc.
- What do you value? For what do you strive?
- Use the SHAPES acronym to journal, writing about one letter each day.
- Give thanks for how God is changing you as you minister to others.
-
-

Unit Four: Building Community Together

- What do you expect to receive from this ministry group?
- Reflect on your gifts and talents. How might they bless your group?

- Describe your most significant interactions with others today.
- Describe the dynamics of your group. Who has power? How is it used? How do people communicate? What roles do people fill?
- Make a list of the people in your urban ministry community. Use the list as a guide for thanksgiving prayer.
- Did you affirm or help someone today? Whom? What was your attitude in that situation?
- Write a letter to someone who has hurt you. Use the exercise to gain perspective and make decisions about what you should do in the reconciliation process.
- Who most challenges your peace and joy when you are with your ministry group? Why? What can be done?
- Who forms the layers of others in your life? List the kinds of people you care about, beginning close, with family and friends. Then move out to the broader world—other Americans, people from other countries, of other economic classes, of other cultures. What is your attitude or responsibility toward others in the world?
- What was the best conversation you had today?
- How effective are your listening skills? Ask God to help you listen closely to others.
-
-

Unit Five: Endings
- What will you be leaving when this adventure ends?
- What have you learned?
- What are your concerns about returning home?
- What have you missed most about home?
- If you could bring one person from this city back home with you, who would it be? Why?
-

More Resources
- Suzan D. Johnson Cook, ed. *Sister to Sister: Devotions for and from African American Women.* Valley Forge, Pa.: Judson Press, 1995.
- Margaret Anne Huffman. *"Through the Valley . . .": Prayers for Violent Times.* Valley Forge, Pa.: Judson Press, 1996.
- Mary L. Mild, ed. *Songs of Miriam: A Women's Book of Devotions.* Valley Forge, Pa.: Judson Press, 1994.
- ——, ed. *Women at the Well: Meditations on Healing and Wholeness.* Valley Forge, Pa.: Judson Press, 1996.

Appendix B
Important Contacts

Name	Phone/Fax/E-mail	Address

Appendix C
Learning Adventures

Date: _____

Team members who visited site:

_____
_____
_____
_____
_____
_____

Name and address of site visited:

_____
_____
_____
_____
_____

Observations (conditions of roads, houses, cars; ethnicity/race of people; places of employment, churches, and social service centers; parks and empty lots; billboards, etc.):

_____
_____
_____
_____
_____
_____
_____
_____
_____
_____
_____
_____
_____

Conversations:

1. _____
   _____
   _____
   _____
   _____
   _____

2. _____
   _____
   _____
   _____
   _____
   _____

3. _____
   _____
   _____
   _____
   _____
   _____

Contact information (addresses, phone numbers):

1. _____
   _____
   _____

2. _____
   _____
   _____

3. _____
   _____
   _____

Appendix D
Learning from Important People and Places

Use the following suggestions to get you started in a new city. Most of these people or places can be found in cities in the United States. Use a phone book to find specifics.

1. Find the Visitor's Bureau or Chamber of Commerce. Pick up brochures and maps, and see how leaders promote the city. Ask the information desk worker or volunteer questions about the city. What's important here? What are significant landmarks? Are there distinct neighborhoods? How could we learn about them?

2. Explore the public library and local bookstores. What local events will be happening during your time in this city? Read public bulletin boards that offer listings of museums, concerts, and lectures. Look for local newsletters or newspapers. Ask a librarian or worker about resources for learning about the area.

3. Ride public transportation. Ride a bus around the city, observing the people who ride with you and the areas the bus drives through. Talk to the person sitting next to you. Ask general questions such as "What is this area like?" and "How is this neighborhood distinct from others?" Some individuals may not be interested in talking with you, but many people will.

4. Call the city's Office of Planning or Map Department and ask for a city neighborhood map. Drive or walk around neighborhood boundaries that are in areas where your group is investing.

5. Talk with neighborhood representatives at community development corporations, tenant boards, activist organizations, or neighborhood planning groups. Sometimes groups like these are listed under neighborhood names in the phone book. Often a call to the Mayor's Office will point you in the right direction.

6. Visit buildings that are open to the public—universities, museums, social service sites, churches, government buildings—and ask for brochures, business cards, or other information about what they do.

7. Choose an area of the city in which you are interested. Drive, or walk, through the area at different times of the day and night—early morning, afternoon, and late evening. Take notes on your observations of neighborhood life. Talk to people when possible.

8. Visit a neighborhood church. See Appendix E for hints about visiting an unfamiliar church.

9. Eat at a neighborhood or ethnic restaurant. Ask the waiter to tell you about the specials. Observe the people who come to the restaurant. Notice how tables are set and how the restaurant is decorated.

Appendix E
Visiting a New Church

You've probably been to church many times. Your home church may be different from this new church you are visiting. There are many ways of worshiping, and this worksheet is designed to help you recognize the cultural aspects of worship. Before you go, reflect on cultural aspects of your home church. Then observe the new church and analyze the same aspects. Try to understand the "why" of culture—why do people dress, sing, or act as they do? What does it mean to them? Why do you respond to it as you do?

Tips for Attending a New Church

Sit with people from the church. If you attend with others in your group, spread out. If you sit together it makes it difficult for people to approach you, and for you to meet new people.

- **Participate.** If people raise their hands in church, try it. If people go forward for prayer at the altar, try it. If people stay at church for an hour after service talking, try it. Your relationships with these Christians will grow as they see you trying to become part of their church.

- **Talk about your experiences.** Do you love hearing two languages in a service? Do you hate having to dress up? Do you disagree with how this church treats women? Do you think its silly to call your pastor "The Reverend Doctor" or irreverent to call him "Juan?" It's OK to react to cultural differences. When you are moved by an experience, positively or negatively, try the following:
  - **Pray.** Submit your experience to God, asking for discernment and understanding.
  - **Be an anthropologist.** Try to understand what people's words and behaviors mean to them. If you can get "inside their heads" to see their worship service from their point of view, you may gain understanding and compassion.
  - **Take risks.** Even if a type of worship is far from your comfort level or past experience, try it. The people in this church worship God in a particular way for a reason. Maybe they are connected to an aspect of God's character that your church doesn't emphasize. Learn from them.
  - **Keep talking about your experience with your group.** There is no "right" way to react to cultural difference. Talk about what is easy for you, what is hard, what seems strange, etc. Use the experience to learn about yourself and others.

Cultural Aspects of Church	Your Home Church	New Church
Sunday morning dress		
Weekday/Sunday evening dress		
Addressing the pastor (Dr./Rev./Pat)		
Addressing other believers (Ms. Jones/Sis. Ann/Ann)		
Order of service (liturgy, altar call, offering, etc.)		
Physical expression during worship		
Physical expression during sermons		
Length of sermon		
Length of service		
Role of women		
Language(s) spoken		
Number of weekly services		
Other:		
Other:		

Appendix F
Personal and Corporate Spiritual Disciplines

1. Read a book on prayer (e.g., *Beginning Prayer* by John Killinger). Choose an approach from the book and practice it for a week. Describe in your journal what you learned from praying in this way.
2. Pray in silence for five minutes every day this week.
3. Pray a short prayer throughout the day (e.g., "Lord Jesus Christ, have mercy on me.") or pray a Scripture verse or just a word.).
4. Set aside one hour this week that will be free of distraction. Use the time for prayer, reading, and meditation.
5. Write out a prayer in your journal.
6. Act, dance, or draw a prayer.
7. Pray in creation. Take a walk. Watch the sun rise or set and meditate on its beauty.
8. Practice intercessory prayer by lifting up people and situations to God. Make a list, a collection of photographs, or a small flip chart as a reminder of what to pray about.
9. Pray for healing for someone you know. If appropriate, lay hands on that person and pray.
10. Pray for your team and your church.
11. Pray before you get out of bed. Give thanks for the day and give it over to God.
12. Pray as you exercise. Choose a partner and exercise/pray together several times.
13. Try a twenty-four hour fast. Skip a meal (or several) and use the time to meditate on Scripture.
14. Fast from negative input for a week. Eliminate negative music, words, or foods.
15. Memorize Scripture.
16. Pray for the Holy Spirit to influence your spirit, thoughts, words, and actions.
17. Really worship in church. Get there early, sit by yourself, go to the altar. Do something new that may enhance your worship.
18. Write an encouraging letter to someone.
19. Do a kind deed for someone without anyone knowing.
20. Participate in a protest that seeks to bring about God's justice.
21. Meditate on a psalm each day.
22. Read Scripture out loud to yourself or to your roommate before falling asleep.
23. Write out a favorite verse and put it in a prominent place (wallet, mirror, dashboard).
24. Share your faith with someone.

25. Give money, food, or resources to someone in need or to another missionary.
26. Listen to the Bible on tape.
27. Sing praises to God instead of grumbling.
28. Spend a period of time with someone else in silence.
29. Take a mini-retreat of silence. Turn off the sound and spend some time alone with God.
30. As a group, share a meal in silence. Serve one another. Enjoy the camaraderie.
31. Ask someone to pray for you and spend time with them in prayer.
32. Use a concordance to do a word study.
33. Read a chapter of Proverbs each day for a month.
34. Write a letter on behalf of someone who needs support.
35. Write a letter to your representative or senator on behalf of an important cause.
36. Look for opportunity to give authentic words of encouragement to people.
37. Do your work with a willing heart. Do more than is required.
38. Give something away.
39. Choose not to buy something that you could afford to buy, and give the money to someone who needs it.
40. Journal about all the things that you see God doing in the world today.
41. Pray to be shown an area in your life that you need to consecrate to God. Ask the Lord how you should respond.
42. Read a daily devotional book.
43. Participate in a worship service and share Communion.
44. Take time to really listen to someone who needs to be heard.
45. Do one of your daily group tasks (e.g., washing the dishes) as a special offering of worship to God.
46. Use the following space to write down additional ideas from books, speakers, churches, and your team:

More Resources
- *The Book of Common Prayer.* New York: Stanford of Swords, 1850.
- John Killinger. *Beginning Prayer.* Nashville: Upper Room Books, 1993.

Appendix G
Transition: The Characteristics of a Transition and Strategies for Coping

Stage 1: Life Before the Transition	**Stage 2:** The Ending
Summary: Life before the transition is generally stable. You know who you are, what you want, and how to get things done. You know how to live without having to think about every decision. People know you and you know where to go to get what you need. Others recognize your pain and joy and are there for you when you need help. You also have people in your life whom you help. You feel good, complete, and in control of yourself, your relationships, and the things you do.	**Summary:** Either positive or negative change brings an ending or a "death" to some aspect of life. This may be an ending to: feeling good, being in control, or being complete in your sense of yourself, your relationships with others, or the things you do. Some of what is important to you is gone. You may lose your sense of well-being. You have to figure out how to bring the really important into the next stage of your life. Negative aspects may occur at the same time a joyous change is occurring.
Characteristics: • feeling at home • being yourself • an established direction • comfortable roles and relationships • regular rituals and routines • doing is automatic • life feels comfortable • the context feels like you belong • time and space are understood • you know what to expect	**Characteristics:** • change/loss of roles and relationships • change/loss of rituals and routines • change/loss of context in which you have known yourself • change/loss in your sense of self • changes in sense of time and space • can involve both positive and negative experiences and emotions • letting go of what is gone • saying good-bye to the old way of life
Coping Strategies: • strategies are established • support network is strong • options are available • resources are known	**Coping Strategies:** • recognize how you cope with endings • identify what you are losing • recognize the transition • name what is happening • create a personal ritual or remembrance • identify what to bring to the new place • plan ahead/maintain connections • choose to trust God and focus on hope • identify expectations • be thankful for what you have had

This chart developed by Margot Eyring from Bridges' model of transitions and Eyring's research on well-being.

Stage 3: The Neutral Zone	Stage 4: The New Beginning
Summary: The in-between time is temporary, but it may last for a long time. It is a time of making a bridge between the old and the new. It may involve both positive and negative emotions and experiences. The challenge is to find ways to be yourself, to have relationships, and to do what God has created you to do in a different "place". This can be a different geographic place, situation, or life experience. Usually, it is a place where you don't feel like you belong for some reason (e.g., lack of cultural knowledge, different values from those around you, or new responsibilities).	**Summary:** You have stopped getting ready and you have stopped living in a temporary place. You have started again. You are able to be yourself in the "new place." You have new relationships and have learned how to stay connected appropriately to old ones. You know how to do things, where to go, what to expect, who to call, how to behave, and how to be. You feel comfortable, more in control, and satisfied with the new situation.
Characteristics: • confusion and distress • loss of the old/not yet the new • emptiness and hope • reorientation and getting ready • exploration and risk • a bridge to be crossed over • energy is required • have to think about what you do • some successes/some failures • expectations are in process	**Characteristics:** • feeling at home • being yourself again • a new start • new roles and relationships • new rituals and routines • doing becomes more automatic • the new feels comfortable • the context feels like you belong • time and space are understood again • you know what to expect
Coping Strategies: • establish a haven of peace • reflect on who God has made you to be • try out some new rituals and routines • network with old and new friends • pray and journal • be intentional about exploring • make your home "your space" • care for your health • be aware of making comparisons • choose to be open and flexible	**Coping Strategies:** • celebrate • remember what God has done and give thanks • create a stone of remembrance • be prepared for the next transition